ISBN 978-0-259-37946-1
PIBN 10814697

1 MONTH OF
FREE
READING

at

www.ForgottenBooks.com

---◇---

By purchasing this book you are eligible for one month membership to ForgottenBooks.com, giving you unlimited access to our entire collection of over 1,000,000 titles via our web site and mobile apps.

To claim your free month visit:

www.forgottenbooks.com/free814697

English
Français
Deutsche
Italiano
Español
Português

www.forgottenbooks.com

Mythology Photography **Fiction**
Fishing Christianity **Art** Cooking
Essays Buddhism Freemasonry
Medicine **Biology** Music **Ancient
Egypt** Evolution Carpentry Physics
Dance Geology **Mathematics** Fitness
Shakespeare **Folklore** Yoga Marketing
Confidence Immortality Biographies
Poetry **Psychology** Witchcraft
Electronics Chemistry History **Law**
Accounting **Philosophy** Anthropology
Alchemy Drama Quantum Mechanics
Atheism Sexual Health **Ancient History**
Entrepreneurship Languages Sport
Paleontology Needlework Islam
Metaphysics Investment Archaeology
Parenting Statistics Criminology
Motivational

THE TRIUMPH:

A COLLECTION OF MUSIC CONTAINING AN

INTRODUCTORY COURSE FOR CONGREGATIONAL SINGING, THEORY OF MUSIC
AND TEACHER'S MANUAL, ELEMENTARY, INTERMEDIATE
AND ADVANCED COURSES,

FOR

SINGING SCHOOLS AND MUSICAL CONVENTIONS

AND

TUNES, HYMNS, ANTHEMS AND CHANTS, FOR CHOIRS.

EDITED BY

GEO. F. ROOT.

CHICAGO:
PUBLISHED BY ROOT & CADY, 67 WASHINGTON STREET.
1868.

PREFACE.

In the first department of the TRIUMPH the effort is made to furnish a means by which any company of people may join in a musical utterance of words, and it is thought that this department will not only promote the object for which it is prepared, but will be useful to teachers in getting up classes, as many learners having made a beginning in this way, will desire to pursue the subject more scientifically, and will go on with the other departments of the book.

In the second department, not only the elementary principles or doctrines are set forth in order, but a mode of teaching those which are most important is proposed.

The third department is called the "Elementary Course," and goes through the major keys without accidentals. The lessons here are intended for the first term of the Singing School.

In the "Intermediate Course," which is the fourth department, accidentals and the relative minor are introduced in lessons which assume such various musical forms as it is believed will make them attractive and useful to singers in the second stage of their musical advancement.

An important feature in these departments will be found in the arrangement by which tunes and other pieces in the body of the book may be used in the Singing School with the lessons, being so prepared that they contain the same kind of difficulties.

The fifth department is called the "Advanced Course," and as its name indicates, is for advanced singers.

Of the Tunes, Hymns, Anthems and Chants, which form the body of the book, it will only be said that they have been prepared with great care, and it is believed will not disappoint the friends of the various authors whose names are found with them. It may here be stated that the editor is responsible for all tunes and other pieces to which no name is attached.

It is unnecessary to specify further the new features of the TRIUMPH. They will be discovered by all who use the book, and will doubtless receive whatever attention and respect they may merit.

The TRIUMPH is peculiarly fortunate in having among its contributors and special friends some prominent musical men in different parts of the country, whose names are here mentioned in the order in which their contributions were received: C. M. Wyman Keene, N. H., H. R. Palmer, Chicago, T. M. Towne, Wisconsin, and J. E. Gould, Philadelphia. It is proper also to mention as being more immediately connected with us, P. P. Bliss, J. R. Murray, and a son of the editor, F. W. Root.

Our obligations are hereby acknowledged to all who have aided us, and especially to Messrs. Mason Brothers, of New York, for copyrights from their books that we are permitted to use.

It is with great pleasure that this opportunity is taken to express the obligations that we, in common with all American composers, teachers and musicians, are under to our beloved Dr. Mason, who has been the chief instrument in the hands of the Divine Providence in placing music, and its universal and intelligent acquirement, in the position it occupies wherever the English language is spoken. If he shall approve the TRIUMPH, we shall have great hope that it will be acceptable and useful to all.

A. D. 1868, by ROOT & CADY, in the District Court of the United States for the Northern District of Illinois.

Geo. F. Root.

INTRODUCTORY COURSE
FOR CONGREGATIONAL SINGING.

LET THE PEOPLE PRAISE THEE, O GOD, LET ALL THE PEOPLE PRAISE THEE. Ps. LXVII.

IF we do a right action, the first effect is upon ourselves, for the exercise of any of the powers of a man is felt first by the man himself. This being true, they are in error who think there is no use in singing unless they can benefit or entertain others: for singing is not only an expression, but an exercise of our emotional nature; and the one who sings, is by this law the first to be affected by the act.

A man then may exercise and strengthen certain good affections in himself, even if he cannot sing well enough to entertain others; indeed, this may be done if he cannot sing any tune at all; for the mere emotional utterance of words that he loves, has the effect to strengthen the affections that they bring into exercise.

In ordinary congregations all could be benefitted by this emotional utterance, if once the idea of musical entertainment could be banished, and musical people would be willing to use simpler modes of utterance.

[It should be said here that singers can bring the best resources of their art to the singing of simple tunes; and every noble heart among them will be glad to do so if it will benefit his neighbor; and on occasions of public worship he will never, for his own particular benefit desire to use a tune so difficult that it will exclude others from participating, for that would be selfish, and utterly opposed to the spirit of our Christian religion.]

Every one has a song voice as well as a speech voice, and when the words we speak are emotional rather than intellectual—of the affection more than of the thought—something of the song-voice comes into them. Every term of endearment to father, mother, brother, sister, wife, child, or friend—every expression of love to the Lord or to the neighbor—has in it that emotional quality, which, carried further, becomes singing.

Another cannot sing our affection for us, for beside the fact that no two have affections exactly alike, it is a work that all may see cannot be done by proxy. Every one, therefore, who wishes to improve his emotional nature must exercise it himself.

Should any congregation desire to try this, a beginning may be made by repeating together, in the ordinary speech voice, the following hymn :—

[It would be well to have a leader who knows something of music, and who, if the people are not supplied with books, may give out the hymns two lines at a time.]

Let the utterance be deliberate and distinct.

1 Let us with a joyful mind,
  Praise the Lord for He is kind :
  For His mercies shall endure,
  Ever faithful, ever sure.

2 He, with all-commanding might,
  Filled the new-made world with light :
  For His mercies shall endure,
  Ever faithful, ever sure.

3 All things living He doth feed ;
  His full hand supplies their need :
  For His mercies shall endure,
  Ever faithful, ever sure.

4 Let us with a joyful mind,
  Praise the Lord, for He is kind :
  For His mercies shall endure,
  Ever faithful, ever sure.

We might derive both benefit and pleasure from uttering in this way such other words as contain and express sentiments that we love, and that we can utter as our own, but we will not stop here, we will try to acquire a form of utterance that will be more emotional, and in which we

3

can more strongly exercise our affections. It must be remembered, however, that no form is useful that requires much thought while we are using it. A man in prayer would be much hindered if he were continually obliged to attend to his posture, or the grammatical structure of his sentences, or the pronunciation of his words; and a singer who is always thinking of his tune or the sound of his voice is in a similar difficulty.

It is true that we have to learn all the forms that we use, but it is equally true that they answer their right purpose only in proportion to the ease and absence of thought with which we use them. What we have done so far, we could do with very little thought, for we are accustomed to this simple utterance of words; the next step, however, will introduce us to a form that we are not accustomed to, and to which we shall have to give more time and practice.

Repeat again this hymn with the ordinary speech voice, but now separate the syllables from each other and give each one with force, being also careful to give each an equal amount of time. If each is also made short, it will aid in keeping the voices together. It may be represented thus :

Let — us, — with — a — joy — ful — mind,
Praise — the — Lord, — for — He — is — kind ;
For — His — mer — cies — shall — en — dure,
Ev — er — faith — ful, — ev — er — sure.
					[Repeat the entire Hymn if the practice is needed.]

If the audience have the words before them, this may be done altogether, (after the leader has given an example); if not, he may give out two lines at a time, as before.

[The leader will remember that this is spoken, not sung.]

What we have now done is not the step we wish to take—only a preparation for it, for this would not be a good form for the expression of either thought or affection.

We will now repeat this hymn again, but this time let us prolong the sound of the vowel in each syllable.

It should here be said that in all words the vowels are the emotional elements, and the consonants the thought elements. If we are speaking to the intellects or reasoning powers of men, we do not dwell on the vowels, but go quick and straight to the consonants. If, on the other hand, we are appealing to their feelings, and trying to draw out their emotions, we unconsciously prolong and dwell upon the vowels. This would be illustrated by the two ways in which we utter the following sentences :—

Intellectual. Two things, each of which is equal to a third, are necessarily equal to each other.
Emotional.				O wondrous power !
						O tender love !
					That brought our Savior from above.

It is hardly necessary to say in this connection that words, to be good for music, must be emotional rather than intellectual.

Let us now repeat this hymn with this same regular movement, but dwell more on the vowel sounds, making the last syllable in each line about twice as long as either of the others. This may be represented thus :—

Let   us   with   a   joy - ful   mind,

Praise the   Lord   for   He   is   kind ;

For   His   mer - cies   shall   en - dure

Ev - er   faith - ful,   ev - er   sure.
					[Continue through the Hymn if thought best.]

[While nothing would be said here about the pitch of the voice, it would be well for the leader in giving the example to take a pitch about D below, and keep it steadily throughout. Most of the audience would unconsciously fall into the same sound.]

Let us now take another hymn, and express it in the same way, only we will all try to give the same sound of voice. It is not necessary to have all the voices at the same sound or pitch, but the natural tendency will be to get together in this respect, and it will be pleasanter to do so.

1 Thou, who art en-throned a - bove, Thou, in whom we live and move ;
2 When the morn - ing paints the skies, When the stars of eve - ning rise,

Sweet it is with joy - ful tongue, To re - sound Thy praise in song.
We Thy prais - es will re-cord, Sov-ereign Ru - ler, might - y Lord.

We have been so accustomed to hear tunes with these hymns, that the monotony of this mode of utterance, although emotional, will prevent its being useful. We will, therefore, vary the sound or pitch of the fifth and sixth syllables in each line. We will make them a little higher than the others. This may be represented thus :—

1 Thou, who art en- throned a - bove, Thou, in whom we live and move;
2 When the morn-ing paints the skies, When the stars of eve - ning rise,

Sweet it is with joy - ful tongue, To re - sound Thy praise in song.
We Thy prais - es will re - cord, Sov-ereign Ru - ler, might - y Lord !

[*May be continued.*]

[The teacher will probably understand that this higher pitch is but one step above the others.]

We will now give another form for the utterance of the first hymn, but it will be easier to tell where these large dots are that note the sounds, if we have a line, on, or above, or below which, we can place them. And now it will not be necessary to print the words higher or lower with the tune, for the dots or notes will show the changes of the words. It should here be said that notes help even those who do not understand music at all, for they are a picture of the tune, and go up or down, or skip around, just as the tune does.

Let us all now join in the next tune, being guided by the notes.

NORTHWEST. 7s.

1 Let us with a joy - ful mind, Praise the Lord for He is kind
2 He, with all com-mand-ing might, Filled the new-made world with light
3 All things liv - ing doth he feed; His full hand sup-plies their need
4 Let us with a joy - ful mind, Praise the Lord for He is kind

For His mer - cies shall en - dure, Ev - er faith - ful, ev - er sure.
For His mer - cies shall en - dure, Ev - er faith - ful, ev - er sure.
For His mer - cies shall en - dure, Ev - er faith - ful, ev - er sure.
For His mer - cies shall en - dure, Ev - er faith - ful, ev - er sure.

In the following hymn we will use a still higher sound; so in the representation we must have another line :—

BLONDEL. 7s.

1 Thou, who art en-throned a - bove, Thou, in whom we live and move ;
2 When the morn - ing paints the skies, When the stars of eve - ning rise,
3 Decks the spring with flowers the field, Har - vest rich doth au - tumn yield ?
4 Sov-ereign Ru - ler I might - y Lord, We thy prais - es will re - cord :

Sweet it is with joy - ful tongue, To re-sound thy praise in song.
We thy prais - es will re - cord, Sov-ereign Ru - ler, might - y Lord !
Giv - er of all good be - low, Lord, from Thee those bless-ings flow.
Giv - er of these bless-ings, we Pour the grate - ful song to Thee.

As soon as a form or tune is acquired so that we can use it without effort; we may commence the work of self-improvement; but if we are not accustomed to fix our minds on the words sung, but are more inclined listen to the tune, we shall find it difficult to concentrate our thoughts we ought.

We shall be like untrained children at school, who are disturbed and distracted by every unusual sight or sound, and must try many times fore we can take the sentiments contained in the words fully into our hear and bear them upon our song unobstructed and unhindered, up to the gr object of all worship.

The following hymns and selections are designed to be sung by *all the people* in *any congregation.* Not one need be silent, who has the power of speech. That some may not get the sound exactly with the others should not prevent them from joining, for in these simple forms a few times trying will remedy that difficulty in almost every case; and if it does not, the worship is so much more important, that the form is of but little consequence in comparison.

ELVIRA. 7s.

1 All ye na - tions praise the Lord! All ye lands your voi - ces raise;
2 For his truth and mer - cy stand, Past, and pres - ent, and to be,

Heaven and earth, with loud ac - cord, Praise the Lord—for ev - er praise!
Like the years of His right hand, Like His own e - ter - ni - ty.

BROOKWELL. 8s & 7s.

1 Hark! what mean those ho - ly voi - ces, Sweet-ly sound - ing through the skies!
2 Hear them tell the won-drous sto - ry, Hear them chant in hymns of joy:
3 "Christ is born, the great A - noint - ed, Heaven and earth His prais - es sing!

Lo! th' an - gel - ic host re - joi - ces; Heavenly hal - le - lu - jahs rise.
"Glo - ry in the high-est, glo - ry! Glo - ry be to God most high!
Oh re - ceive whom God ap - point-ed For your Proph-et, Priest and King!

ST. GEORGE. L. M.

1 From all that dwell be-low the skies, Let the Cre - a - tor's praise a - rise;
2 E - ter - nal are Thy mer-cies Lord, E - ter - nal truth at-tends Thy word:

Let the Re-deem-er's name be sung, Thro' ev-ery land, by ev-ery tongue.
Thy praise shall sound from shore to shore, Till suns shall rise and set no more.

WHITEWATER. S. M.

1 Oh, bless the Lord, my soul! Let all with - in - me join,
2 Oh, bless the Lord, my soul! Nor let His mer - cies lie
3 'T is He for - gives thy sins; 'T is He re - lieves thy pain;

And aid my tongue to bless His name, Whose fa-vors are di - vine.
For - got - ten in un-thank - ful - ness, And with-out prais - es die.
'T is He that heals thy sick - ness - es, And makes thee young a - gain.

GRETRY. 8s & 7s.

1 Sav - ior, breathe an eve - ning bless-ing, Ere re - pose our spir-its seal:
2 Tho' de - struc-tion walk a - round us, Tho' the ar - row near us fly,
3 Tho' the night be dark and drea - ry, Dark-ness can not hide from Thee;
4 Should swift death this night o'er-take us, And our couch be-come our tomb,

Sin and want we come on - foss - ing; Thou canst save, and thou canst heal.
An - gel guards from thee sur - round us; We are safe, if thou art nigh.
Thou art He who, nev - er wea - ry, Watch-eth where Thy peo-ple lie.
May the morn in heav-en a - wake us, Clad in light and death-less bloom

HALCYON. S. M.

1 How gen - tle God's com - mands! How kind His pre - cepts are!
2 Be - neath His watch - ful eye His saints se - cure - ly dwell;
3 Why should this anx - ious load Press down your wea - ry mind?
4 His good - ness stands ap - proved, Un-changed from day to day;

Come, cast your bur - dens on the Lord, And trust His con-stant care.
That hand which bears all na - ture up, Shall guard His chil - dren well.
Haste to your heaven-ly Fa-ther's throne, And sweet re-fresh-ment find.
I'll drop my bur - den at His feet, And bear a song a - way.

MYRTLE HILL. S. M.

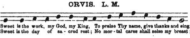

1 While my Re - deem - er's near, My shep - herd and my guide,
2 To ev - er fra - grant meads, Where rich a - bun - dance grows,
3 Dear Shep - herd, if I stray, My wander-ing feet re - store ;

I bid fare - well to anx - ious fear ; My wants are all sup - plied.
His gra - cious hand in - dul - gent loads, And guards my sweet re - pose.
To Thy fair pas - tures guide my way, And let me rove no more.

LAUREL WOOD. C. M.

1 Our Father, God, who art in heav - en, All hal-lowed be Thy name !
2 Give us, this day, our dai - ly bread, And, as we those for - give
3 In - to temp - ta - tion lead us not ; From e - vil set us free ;

Thy king - om come ; Thy will be done, In earth and heaven the same !
Who sin a - gainst us, so may we For - giv - ing grace re - ceive.
And thine the king - dom, thine the power And glo - ry, ev - er be.

We have here a higher sound, and in the representation will use another line.

ODA. C. M.

1 Oh, that the Lord would guide my ways, To keep His stat - utes still !
2 Oh, send Thy Spir - it down, to write Thy law up - on my heart ;
3 Or - der my foot - steps by Thy word, And make my heart sin-cere ;
4 Make me to walk in Thy com - mands, 'T is a de - light-ful road ;

Oh that my God would give me grace To know and do His will.
Nor let my tongue in - dulge de - ceit, Nor act the li - ar's part.
Let sin have no do - min - ion, Lord, But keep my con-science clear,
Nor let my head, nor heart, nor hands, Of - fend a-gainst my God.

Where two words are sung to one note, they are uttered quicker

ORVIS. L. M.

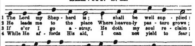

1 Sweet is the work, my God, my King, To praise Thy name, give thanks and sing,
2 Sweet is the day of sa - cred rest ; No mor - tal cares shall seize my breast ;

To show Thy love by morn-ing light, And talk of all Thy truth at night.
Oh, may my heart in tune be found, Like Da-vid's harp of sol-emn sound.

LEAVITT. S. M.

1 The Lord my Shep - herd is ; I shall be well sup - plied :
2 He leads me to the place Where heaven-ly pas - ture grows ;
3 If e'er I go a - stray, He doth my soul re - claim :
4 While He af - fords His aid, I can not yield to fear ;

Since He is mine and I am His, What can I want be - side.
Where liv - ing wa - ters gent - ly pass, And full sal - va - tion flows.
And guides me in His own right way, For His most ho - ly name.
Tho' I should walk thro' death's dark shade, My Shep-herd's with me there.

PALMTREE. S. M.

1 We lift our hearts to Thee, Thou Day - star from on high ;
2 Oh, let Thy ris - ing beams Dis - pel the shades of night ;
3 How beau - teous na - ture now ! How dark and sad be - fore !
4 May we this life im - prove, To mourn for er - rors past ;

The sun it - self is but Thy shade, Yet cheers both earth and sky.
And let the glo - ries of Thy love, Come like the morn - ing light !
With joy we view the pleas - ing change, And na-ture's God a - dore.
And live this short, re - volv - ing day As if it were our last.

ROWENA. L. M.

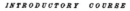

1 Soon may the last glad song a - rise, Thro' all the mil-lions of the skies.
2 Let thrones and powers and king-doms be O - be - dient, might-y God, to Thee !
3 Oh, let that glo-rious an-them swell, Let host to host the tri-umph tell,

That song of tri-umph which re-cords That all the earth is now the Lord's!
And, o - ver land and stream and main, Wave Thou the scep-ter of Thy reign!
That not one reb - el heart re-mains, But o - ver all the Sav - ior reigns!

SABERTON. 7s.

1 Songs of praise the an - gels sang, Heaven with hal - le - lu - jahs rang,
2 Songs of praise a - woke the morn, When the Prince of Peace was born :
3 Heaven and earth shall pass a - way ; Songs of praise shall crown the day :
4 Saints be - low, with heart and voice, Still in songs of praise re - joice ;

When Je - ho - vah's work be - gun, When He spake, and it was done.
Songs of praise a - rose when He Cap - tive led cap - tiv - i - ty.
God will make new heavens and earth; Songs of praise shall hail their birth.
Learn-ing here by faith and love, Songs of praise to sing a - bove.

PINE GROVE. C. M.

1 How sweet, how heaven-ly is the sight, When those who love the Lord
2 When each can feel his broth-er's sigh, And with him bear a part!
3 When, free from en - vy, scorn and pride, Our wish - es all a - bove,

In one an - oth - er's peace de-light, And so ful - fil His word!
When sor-row flows from eye to eye, And joy from heart to heart.
Each can his broth-er's fail - ings hide, And show a broth-er's love.

EVERHART. 7s.

1 Sons of Zi - on, raise your songs! Praise to Zi - on's King be - longs ;
2 Sore the strife, but rich the prize, Pre-cious in the Vic-tor's eyes ;
3 Sing we then the Vic-tor's praise; Go ye forth and strew the ways;
4 Place the crown up - on His brow; Ev - ery knee to Him shall bow;

His the Vic-tor's crown and fame: Glo - ry to the Sav - ior's name!
Glo-rious is the work a-chieved, Sa - tan van-quished, man *re - lieved!
Bid Him wel - come to His throne; He is wor - thy, He a - lone!
Him the bright-est ser - aph sings; Heaven proclaims Him "King of kings!"

TRUCE. C. M.

1 O God, my heart is ful - ly bent To mag - ni - fy Thy name;
2 To all the listen-ing tribes, O Lord, Thy won-ders I will tell;
3 Be-cause Thy mer - cy's bound-less height The high-est heaven tran-scends.
4 Be thou, O God, ex - al - ted high A - bove the star - ry frame;

My tongue, with cheer-ful songs of praise, Shall cel - e - brate Thy fame.
And to those na - tions sing Thy praise That round a - bout us dwell.
And far be-yond th' as - pi - ring clouds Thy faith - ful truth ex - tends.
And let the world with one con - sent, Con - fess Thy glo - rious name.

GUEST. C. M.

1 O hap - py land! O hap - py land! Where saints and an - gels dwell;
2 But ev - ery voice in yon - der throng On earth has breathed a prayer;
3 Thou heaven-ly Friend! Thou heavenly Friend! Oh, hear us when we pray!

We long to join that glo-rious band, And all their an-thems swell.
No lips un-taught can join that song, Or learn the mu - sic there.
Now let Thy par - doning grace de-scend, And take our sins a - way.

When two syllables are printed under one note, they are to be sung quicker. They are to take as much time only as one syllable in the other places.

BERRINGTON. 11s & 10s.

1	Bright - est and	best	of the	sons	of the	morn - ing!
2	Cold	on his	cra - dle the	dew -	drops are	shin - ing,
3	Say,	shall we	yield	him, in	cost - ly de -	vo - tion,
4	Vain -	ly we	of - fer each	am -	ple ob -	la - tion,
5	Bright - est and	best	of the	sons	of the	morn - ing!

Dawn	on our	dark - ness and	lend	us thine	aid ;
Low	lies his	Head	with the	beasts	of the	stall :
O -	dors of	E - dom and	of -	ferings di -	vine?
Vain	ly with	gold	would His	fa -	vors se - cure ;
Dawn	on our	dark - ness and	lend	us thine	aid ;

Star	of the	East,	the ho -	ri -	zon a -	dorn - ing,
An -	gels a -	dore	Him in	slum -	ber re -	clin - ing,
Gems	of the	moun - tain, and	pearls	of the	o - cean,
Rich -	er, by	far,	is the	heart's a -	do -	ra - tion,
Star	of the	East,	the ho -	ri -	zon a -	dorn - ing,

Guide	where our	in -	fant Re -	deem -	er is	laid.
Ma -	ker, and	Mon -	arch, and	Sav -	ior of	all !
Myrrh	from the	for -	est, or	gold	from the	mine?
Dear -	er to	God	are the	prayers	of the	poor.
Guide	where our	in -	fant Re -	deem -	er is	laid.

OLOFF. S. M.

1	Is	this	the	kind re - turn?	Are these the thanks we owe?
2	To	what	a	stub - born frame	Hath sin re - duced our mind?
3	Turn,	turn	us, might - y God,	And mold our souls a - fresh;
4	Let	past in - grat - i - tude,	Pro - voke our weep - ing eyes,

Thus to a - buse e - ter - nal Love, Whence all our bless - ings flow !
What strange, re-bel - lious wretch - es we ! And God as strange-ly kind !
Break Sov-ereign Grace ! these hearts of stone, And give us hearts of flesh.
And hour - ly, as new mer - cies fall, Let hour - ly thanks a - rise.

CAPULET. 8s & 7s, Double.

1 Glo-rious things of thee are spo - ken, Zi - on, cit - y of our God!
2 On the Rock of A - ges found - ed, What can shake her own re-pose?

He whose word can ne'er be bro - ken, Chose thee for his own a - bode.
With sal - va - tion's wall sur-round - ed, She can smile at all her foes.

Lord, Thy church is still Thy dwell - ing, Still is pre - cious in Thy sight;
Glo-rious things of Thee are spo - ken, Zi - on, cit - y of our God;

Ju - dah's tem - ple far ex - cel - ling, Beam-ing with the gos - pel's light.
He whose word can ne'er be bro - ken, Chose thee for His own a - bode.

TELFORD. 8s & 5.

1 Sing of Je - sus, sing for - ev - er, Of the love that chang-es
2 Thro' the des - ert drear He leads them, With the bread of heaven He
3 There they see the Lord who bought them, Him who came from heaven, and
4 Sing of Je - sus, sing for - ev - er, Sing the love that chang-es

nev - er: Who or what can from Him sev - er, Those He makes His own?
feeds them, And thro' all the way He speeds them To their homes a - bove.
sought them, Him who by His spir - it taught them, Him they serve and love.
nev - er: Who or what can from Him sev - er, Those He makes His own?

KINSIE. 7s & 5s.

RECTOR. 7s & 6s.

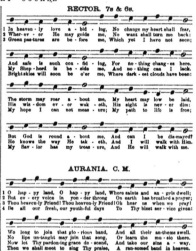

1 On - ward speed thy con-quering flight, An - gel, on - ward speed!
2 On - ward speed thy con-quering flight, An - gel, on - ward fly!
3 On - ward speed thy con-quering flight, An - gel, on - ward speed!

Cast a - broad thy ra - diant light, Bid the shades re - cede;
Long has been the reign of night, Bring the morn - ing nigh:
Morn-ing bursts up - on our sight. Lo! the time de - creed:

Tread the i - dols in the dust, Heath - en fanes de - stroy;
Un - to thee earth's suf - ferers, lift Their im - plo - ring wail;
Now the Lord His king - dom takes, Thrones and em - pires fall;

Spread the gos - pel's love and trust, Spread the gos - pel's joy.
Bear them heav - en's ho - ly gift, Ere their cour - age fail.
Now the joy - ous song a - wakes, "God is All in All!"

1 In heaven - ly love a - bid - ing, No change my heart shall fear,
2 Wher- ev - er He may guide me, No wants shall turn me back:
3 Green pas-tures are be - fore me, Which yet I have not seen;

And safe is such con - fid - ing, For no - thing chang - es here.
My Shep - herd is be - side me, And no - thing can I lack.
Bright skies will soon be o'er me, Where dark - est clouds have been:

The storm may roar a - bout me, My heart may low be laid,
His wis - dom ev - er wak - eth, His sight is nev - er dim:
My hope I can not meas - ure; My path to life is free;

But God is round a - bout me, And can I be dis-mayed?
He knows the way He tak - eth, And I will walk with Him.
My Sav - ior has my treas - ure, And He will walk with me.

FARWELL. 8s, 7s & 4.

AURANIA. C. M.

1 Ev - ery hu - man tie may per - ish; Friend to friend un - faith - ful
2 In the fur - nace God may prove thee, Thence to bring thee forth more

prove; Moth-ers cease their own to cher - ish; Heaven and earth at last
bright; But can nev - er cease to love thee; Thou art pre-cious in

re - move: But no chang - es Can a - vert a Fa - ther's love.
His sight: God is with thee; God, thine ev - er - last - ing light.

1 O hap - py land, O hap - py land, Where saints and an - gels dwell;
2 But ev - ery voice in yon - der throng On earth has breathed a prayer;
3 Thou heaven-ly Friend! Thou heaven-ly Friend! Oh hear us when we pray!
4 Be all our fresh, our youth-ful days To Thy blest ser - vice given!

We long to join that glo - rious band, And all their an-thems swell.
No lips un-taught may join that song, Or learn the mu - sic there.
Now let Thy pardon-ing grace de - scend, And take our sins a - way.
Then we shall meet to sing Thy praise, A ran-somed band in heaven.

WITHINGTON. 8s & 7s, Peculiar.

1 God is our ref - uge ev - er near, Our help in trib - u - la - tion;
2 The stream that flows from Zi - on's hill, Shall yet, se - rene - ly glid - ing,

There-fore His peo - ple shall not fear A - mid a wreck'd cre - a - tion;
With joy the ho - ly cit - y fill, His pres-ence there a - bid - ing;

Tho' moun-tains from their base be hurled, And o - cean shake the sol - id
The Lord, her glo - ry and de - fense, Will guard his cho - sen res - i -

world, The Lord is our sal - va - tion, The Lord is our sal - va - tion.
dence, His time - ly aid pro - vid - ing, His time - ly aid pro - vid - ing.

CLEAR LAKE. 6s & 4s.

1 God bless our na - tive land, Firm may she ev - er stand,
2 For her our prayer shall rise, To God, a - bove the skies.

Thro' storm and night; When wild the temp - ests rave, Ru - ler of
On Him we wait: Thou who art ev - er nigh, Guard-ing with

wind and wave, Do Thou our coun - try save, By Thy great might.
watch - ful eye, To Thee a - loud we cry, God save the State!

WINONA. 8s & 6s.

1 Let ev - ery heart re - joice and sing; Let cho - ral an - theme
2 He bids the sun to rise and set; In heaven His power is

rise; Ye rev - erend men and chil-dren, bring To God your sac -
known. And earth sub - dued to Him, shall yet Bow low be - fore

ri - fice: For He is good,—the Lord is good, And kind are
His throne: For He is good,—the Lord is good, And kind are

all His ways: With songs and hon - ors sound - ing loud, The Lord
all His ways: With songs and hon - ors sound - ing loud, The Lord

Je - ho - vah praise; While the rocks and the rills, While the vales
Je - ho - vah praise; While the rocks and the rills, While the vales

and the hills, A glo - rious an - them raise, Let each pro - long
and the hills, A glo - rious an - them raise, Let each pro - long

the grate - ful song, And the God of our fa - thers praise.
the grate - ful song, And the God of our fa - thers praise.

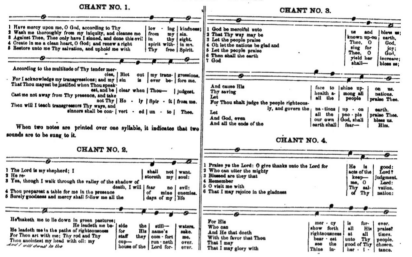

CHANT NO. 1.

1 Have mercy upon me, O God, according to Thy	lov - ing	kindness;
2 Wash me thoroughly from my iniquity, and cleanse me	from	my	sin.
3 Against Thee, Thee only have I sinned, and done this evil	in	thy	sight.
4 Create in me a clean heart, O God; and renew a right	spirit with-	in me.
5 Restore unto me Thy salvation, and uphold me with	Thy	free	Spirit.

According to the multitude of Thy tender mer-
     cies, | Blot out | my trans- | gressions.
For I acknowledge my transgressions; and my | sin is | ever be- | fore me.
That Thou mayest be justified when Thou speak-
     est, and be | clear when | Thou— | judgest.
Cast me not away from Thy presence, and take
     not Thy | Ho - ly | Spir - it | from me.
Then will I teach transgressors Thy ways, and
     sinners shall be con- | vert - ed | un - to | Thee.

When two notes are printed over one syllable, it indicates that two sounds are to be sung to it.

CHANT NO. 2.

1 The Lord is my shepherd; I	shall	not	want.
2 He re-	storeth	my	soul:
3 Yes, though I walk through the valley of the shadow of death, I will	fear	no	evil:
4 Thou preparest a table for me in the presence	of	mine	enemies.
5 Surely goodness and mercy shall follow me all the	days of my	life

He maketh me to lie down in green pastures;
     He leadeth me be- | side the | still— | waters.
He leadeth me in the paths of righteousness | for | His | name's | sake.
For Thou art with me; Thy rod and Thy | staff they | com - fort | me.
Thou anointest my head with oil: my | cup— | run - neth | over.
And I will dwell in the | house of the | Lord for- | ever.

CHANT NO. 3.

1 God be merciful unto	us	and	bless us;
2 That Thy way may be	known up-on	earth,
3 Let the people praise	Thee, O	God,
4 Oh let the nations be glad and	sing for	joy;
5 Let the people praise	Thee, O	God,
6 Then shall the earth	yield her	increase;
7 God	shall—	bless us;

And cause His | face to | shine up- | on us.
Thy saving | health a- | mong all | nations.
Let | all the | people | praise Thee.
For Thou shalt judge the people righteous-
     ly, and govern the | na - tions | up - on | earth.
Let | all the | peo - ple | praise Thee.
And God, even | our own | God, shall | bless us.
And all the ends of the | earth shall | fear— | Him.

CHANT NO. 4.

1 Praise ye the Lord: O give thanks unto the Lord for	He is	good:
2 Who can utter the mighty	acts of the	Lord?
3 Blessed are they that	keep-	judgment.
4 Remember	me, O	Lord:
5 O visit me with	Thy sal-	vation.
6 That I may rejoice in the gladness	of Thy	nation.

For His | mer - cy | is | for- | ever.
Who can | show forth | all His | praise?
And He that doeth | righteousness | at all | times.
With the favor that Thou | bear - est | unto Thy | people.
That I may | see the | good of Thy | chosen.
That I may glory with | Thine in- | her - i - | tance.

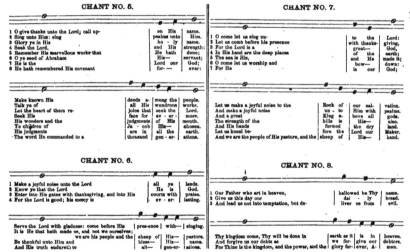

CHANT NO. 5.

1 O give thanks unto the Lord; call up- | on His | name.
2 Sing unto Him: sing | psalms unto | Him.
3 Glory ye in His | ho - ly | name.
4 Seek the Lord, | and His | strength:
5 Remember His marvellous works that | He hath | done;
6 O ye seed of Abraham | His— | servant;
7 He is the | Lord our | God;
8 He hath remembered His covenant | for- — | ever:

Make known His | deeds a- | mong the | people.
Talk ye of | all His | wondrous | works.
Let the heart of them re- | joice that | seek the | Lord.
Seek His | face for | ev - er - | more.
His wonders and the | judgments | of His | mouth.
Ye children of | Ja - cob | His— | chosen.
His judgments | are in | all the | earth.
The word He commanded to a | thousand | gen - er- | ations.

CHANT NO. 6.

1 Make a joyful noise unto the Lord | all ye | lands.
2 Know ye that the Lord | He is | God.
3 Enter into His gates with thanksgiving, and into His | courts with | praise.
4 For the Lord is good; his mercy is | ev - er- | lasting.

Serve the Lord with gladness: come before His | pres-ence | with— | singing.
It is He that hath made us, and not we ourselves;
   we are his people and the | sheep of | His— | pasture.
Be thankful unto Him and | bless— | His— | name.
And His truth endureth to | all— | gen-er- | ations.

CHANT NO. 7.

1 O come let us sing un- | to the | Lord:
2 Let us come before His presence | with thanks- | giving,
3 For the Lord is a | great— | God,
4 In His hand are the deep places | of the | earth;
5 The sea is His, | and He | made it;
6 O come let us worship and | bow— | down:
7 For He | is our | God;

Let us make a joyful noise to the | Rock of | our sal- | vation.
And make a joyful noise | un - to | Him with | psalms.
And a great | King a- | bove all | gods.
The strength of the | hills is | His— | also.
And His hands | formed | the dry | land.
Let us kneel be- | fore the | Lord our | Maker.
And we are the people of His pasture, and the | sheep of | His— | hand.

CHANT NO. 8.

1 Our Father who art in heaven, | hallowed be Thy | name.
2 Give us this day our | dai - ly | bread.
3 And lead us not into temptation, but de- | liver us from | evil.

Thy kingdom come, Thy will be done in | earth as it | is in | heaven.
And forgive us our debts as | we for- | give our | debtors.
For Thine is the kingdom, and the power, and the | glory for- | ever, A- | men.

ANTHEM, NO. 1. Blessed is the People.

ANTHEM, NO. 2. Bless the Lord.

THEORY OF MUSIC,
AND TEACHER'S MANUAL.

CHAPTER I.
GENERAL VIEW OF THE SUBJECT.

I. A musical sound is called a

TONE.

II. Every tone has three properties, viz.:

LENGTH, PITCH, POWER.

[If either of these properties could be taken away from a tone, it would cease to exist. It is therefore necessary, in written music, in order to represent a tone, to have something to stand for its length, and to have something to stand for its pitch, and something to stand for its power: and it will be easily seen that no representation of a tone can be complete, that does not provide for all these things.]

III. There are different lengths of tones, there are different pitches of tones, and different degrees of power of tones. We may take any one pitch and any one degree of power, and practice different lengths; or we may take one length and one degree of power, and practice different pitches; or we may take one length and one pitch, and practice different degrees of power: and thus, although we must have the three properties, length, pitch and power, in every tone we make, we may give more prominence to one or the other, as our musical progress may require.

IV. It might be supposed from the foregoing, that music would naturally divide itself into three departments—one in which the length of tones is the principal thing, one in which the pitch of tones is the principal thing, and one in which power of tones is the principal thing. This is the fact—and all that relates to the length of tones whether in music written or performed, is in a department called *Rhythmics*, and all that relates to the pitch of tones is in a department called *Melodics*, and all that relates to the power of tones is in a department called *Dynamics*.

RHYTHMICS. MELODICS. DYNAMICS.

[It will thus be readily understood, that when we speak of the rhythmic character of a piece of music, we have reference to the time or different lengths of tones employed; and when we speak of its melodic character, we refer to some of the many things relating to pitch; and when we speak of its dynamic character, we refer to differences of power or strength.]

V. There is another thing about tones that does not seem really to belong to either of those departments, and which, perhaps, should have a department by itself. It is called

QUALITY OF TONE.

[The tone of a flute is of one quality, the tone of a violin is of another quality, the tone of a trumpet another, and so on. All may sound together, each producing a tone of exactly the same length, exactly the same pitch, and exactly the same power —and yet a difference will be distinctly perceived.]

VI. Different qualities of tone are needed to express the different emotions that man experiences; and there are, and of course must be, just as many "qualities of tone" as there are kinds of emotions; for tones are the sounds or outward manifestations of emotions, and the voice can produce as great a variety of tones as to quality, as the heart can experience as to emotions, each emotion having its own peculiar sound.

What is a musical sound called? How many properties has a tone? What are they? Can a tone exist without length? Can it exist without pitch? Can it exist without power? How many departments are

*there in music?   What is the first?   The second?   The third?!
In which department is the length of tones studied?   In which is the
pitch of tones studied?   In which the power of tones?   When we
speak of the rhythmic character of a piece of music what do we refer
to?   When we speak of its melodic character to what do we refer?
When we speak of its dynamic character to what?   What is another
thing about tones that is worthy of attention?   Are the sounds produced
by different instruments alike or different as to quality?   How many
qualities of tone can be produced by the human voice?*

CHAPTER II.

RHYTHMICS, NOTES AND RESTS.

VII. If you make a succession of sounds, about as fast as the pulse
beats, they may be represented by characters called

QUARTER NOTES.

[This being the easiest length to sing, the quarter note is the standard from
which we reckon and practice.]
[Take the pitch G for these exercises in Rhythmics.]

VIII. Sounds, each twice as long as a quarter note, are represented by

HALF NOTES.

IX. Sounds, each three times as long as a quarter note, are represented by

DOTTED HALF NOTES.

X. Sounds, each four times as long as a quarter note, are represented by

WHOLE NOTES.

XI. Sounds, each six times as long as a quarter note, are represented by

DOTTED WHOLE NOTES.

XII. The following table gives the notes that stand for sounds, half
and quarter as long as those represented by quarter notes, with their names:

Quarter notes,

Eighth notes,

Sixteenth notes,

XIII. A DOTTED QUARTER NOTE is as long as three eighth notes, and
and a DOTTED EIGHTH is as long as three sixteenths.

[Here, only the length or time of the tones is represented; there is no representation of any particular pitch or degree of power. The note, when it stands
alone, is not enough to represent all the properties of a tone, for, although by it
you can tell how long, it gives you no idea how high or low, or how loud to sing.]

XIV. If any of these sounds are sung, (and they may be, to " la," or
any other syllable,) care should be taken to have the breath well taken, the
tone freely given out, the vowel sound right, the consonant well emitted,
and the pitch and power kept equal and steady.

XV. The first *quality of tone* to be made use of, is that which is most
favorable for giving out the voice or delivering it well, and this is necessa-

rily not very emotional; for the great object at first is to utter sounds and syllables, and without obstruction caused by any wrong position of the vocal organs.

Of course, this involves taking the breath fully, using it economically, and using the right muscles both in taking and giving it out? It involves, also, opening the mouth according to the vowel or word you utter, so that the lips, mouth and tongue will not offer any unnecessary hindrance to the coming out of the tone, and also such a position of the throat as will not be either pinched up or choked on the one side, nor distended and cavernous on the other.

XVI. A figure three (3) placed over or under any three equal notes reduces the length represented by them to that of two of the same kind without the figure. Notes thus written are called TRIPLETS.

XVII. If you were to sing an exercise like the one indicated in paragraph VII, only passing in silence the time of some of the quarter notes, such silence might be indicated by

QUARTER RESTS.

XVIII. There are as many kinds of rests as there are kinds of notes.

Dotted Whole.   Whole.   Dotted Half.   Half.

Dotted Quarter.   Quarter.   Dotted Eighth.   Eighth.

Sixteenth.

XIX. Each rest occupies as much time as its corresponding note in the same piece.

[There are other notes and rests such as Double, Thirty-seconds, Sixty-fourths, &c., but they are seldom used.]

2

The following table shows all the notes in common use.

What are the characters called that represent the length of sounds? What kind of notes stand for that length which is the easiest to sing? What kind of notes stand for sounds twice this length, or, in common language, What kind of notes are twice as long as quarter notes? . What kind of notes are three times as long? What kind of notes are four times as long? What six times? What kind of notes are half as long as quarters? What are a quarter as long? How many sixteenths are equal to an eighth? How many to a dotted eighth? How many sixteenths to a quarter? To a dotted quarter? To a half? To a dotted half? To a whole? To a dotted whole? How many eighths are equal to a quarter? A half, &c., [and so on with quarters and miscellaneously.)   How does the figure 3 affect a group of notes? What is such a group called?   Can you tell by a note alone how high or how low to sing?   Can you tell how loud or how soft?   What one thing does the note alone stand for?   In singing, should the breath be fully or partially taken?   Should the mouth be opened so as to give out the sound freely?   Should you stoop or be erect?   What are the names of those characters which stand for silence while you are performing a piece of music? How many kinds of rests are there?   How are they named?   In which department have you been studying in this chapter—Rhythmics, Melodics, or Dynamics?

CHAPTER III.

MEASURES, BEATING TIME AND ACCENTS.

XX. Count one, two; one, two; one, two; one, two; several times, evenly and steadily, about as fast as you sang the quarter notes. This process is called measuring time, and each one, two, is said to be a MEASURE. A measure with two parts is called DOUBLE MEASURE.

XXI. You may measure time by motions of the hand—indeed, this is the common way while singing, and each two motions will manifest a measure. The motions are usually down, up. These should always be prompt, the hand resting, if necessary, at the point where it stops.

XXII. Now, sing quarter notes to the syllable " la," and move the hand, or " beat time," while you sing.

This may be represented thus:

La, la,   la, la,   la, la,   la, la,   la, la,   la, la,   la, la.
Firm-ly now each voice is   ring-ing, While to-geth-er   all are sing-ing.

XXIII. The little upright lines are called bars, and the spaces between them are called measures. The two bars at the close, form what is called a double bar. Notice that the portions of time that you measure with the counts, or beats, are the real measures.

[These spaces between the bars in which the notes are written are only signs of measures, but for brevity are usually called measures—just as you say that this, $100, is a hundred dollars, when it is only its sign.]

XXIV. Now, sing six quarter notes (three measures), and then a tone as long as two beats, or a whole measure. Do this twice, making eight measures in all.

This would be represented thus:

La, la,   la, la,   la, la,   la,   la, la,   la, la,   la, la,   la.
Come ye   tim - id   ones draw near, There is naught to dread or   fear.

XXV. Count one, two, three; one, two, three; one, two, three; several times, evenly and steadily, about as fast as before. This is measuring time again, but now our measures have three parts instead of two, and are called TRIPLE MEASURES.

XXVI. The motions of the hand in beating triple time, are down, left, up.

XXVII. Sing four triple measures, one sound to each beat. That would be represented thus:

La, la,   la,   la, la,   la,   la, la,   la,   la, la,   la.
Cheer - ful - ly,   Care - ful - ly,   Hope - ful - ly,   Joy - ful - ly.

XXVIII. Sing four measures again, but now put a half and quarter note in each measure.

La,   la, la,   la, la,   la, la,   la.
O   how long   the way   we're go - ing.

XXIX. Now, four measures again, but with a dotted half in each.

La,   la,   la,   la.
How   slow,   we   go.

XXX. Count one, two, three, four, several times, evenly and steadily as before. These are QUADRUPLE MEASURES.

XXXI. The motions of the hand for this kind of time, or measure, are down, left, right, up.

XXXII.

La, la, la, la, la, la, la, la, la, la, la, la.
Ev-'ry step that we are tak-ing, Shows some prog-ress we are mak-ing.

XXXIII. Four measures again, but now a half and two quarters in each measure.

La, la, la, la, la, la, la, la, la, la, la, la.
Half, quar-ter, half, quar-ter, half, quar-ter, half, quar-ter.

XXXIV. Now, a dotted half and a quarter in each measure.

La, la, la, la, la, la, la, la.
Help me, help me, sing this long note.

XXXV. Now fill each measure with a single sound

La, la, la, la.
Whole note; long sound.

XXXVI. Measures with six counts, or beats, are called SEXTUPLE MEASURES.

XXXVII. The beats for sextuple measures are, down, down, left, right, up, up.

La, la, la, la, la, la, la, la, la, la, la, la.
Long-est of meas-ures this one of the six parts is.

XXXVIII. Now three quarters and a dotted half in each.

La, la, la, la, la, la, la, la, la, la, la, la, la, la, la, la.
O come and sing, Friends one and all, Sweet voices bring Quick to the call.

XXXIX. Now fill each measure with a single sound.

La, la, la, la.
Oh slow, We go.

[In any of the foregoing kinds of measures, we may have eighths by singing two sounds to a beat; triplets, by singing three; sixteenths, by singing four, &c.]

XL. In any kind of measure we naturally give more strength to the first part. This is called

ACCENT.

XLI. In quadruple measure there is a lesser accent also upon the third part; and in sextuple upon the fourth part.

[In order to make the accent of the music agree with the accent of the words, when the words begin with an unaccented syllable, the music has to commence on the last part of the measure. In such cases, the last measure of the piece always lacks as much time as is used before the time.]

XLII. When a tone begins upon an unaccented part of the measure, and continues through an accented part, the natural accent is set aside, and a new accent given, called

SYNCOPATION.

[The natural accent is, by the rules of good taste, often set aside, and it is rarely well to make it prominent for any length of time.]

[In the foregoing lessons, attention should not only be paid to the rhythmic idea, which is the prominent one, but to breathing, delivering the tone, enunciation and pronunciation, and so begin at the right place, the cultivation of the voice.]

How many kinds of measures have we learned? How did we at first manifest them? By what other mode, beside counting, can they be manifested or marked? What kind of measure has two parts, and is manifested by two counts, or beats? How are the beats made? What kind has three parts? (and so on through all.) What are the little upright lines called? What the two at the close of each lesson? What are the spaces between the bars in which the notes are written called? Which are the real measures, those written in the books, or those manifested by counts, or beats? Which are the signs of measures? In beating time, which are better, sluggish or prompt motions? How many quarter notes will fill a measure in double time? How many in triple? (and so on) What one note will fill a measure in double time? What one in triple? (and so on.) What two will fill a measure in triple time? What two in quadruple? What other two? (and so on.) How many eighths would be required to fill a measure in double time? (and so on.) What is that stress of voice called which we apply to certain parts of the measure? Where does this accent naturally fall in double measure? In triple? (and so on.) What is that accent called which is given to a tone when it commences upon the unaccented part of a measure, and continues through the accented part? What should our position be while we are singing? (and so on about cultivation of the voice.) In which department have we here been studying—Rhythmics, Melodics, or

CHAPTER IV.

THE STAFF.

[The study of Melodics, or the pitch of sounds, usually commences with C; but G is better, because it is nearer the pitch of voice, and thus easier for those whose voices are not true, and also because having been practicing in Rhythmics at that pitch, the pupils will be more likely to give it in tune.]

XLIII. We have named the different *lengths* of tones by the different names of notes. Their pitches are named by letters. The pitch we have been using is named G.

[The teacher here sings G, F, E, D and C—first with "la," and then with syllables sol, fa mi, re, do. It will be a good plan for the class to do the same, and then name the pitches as he sings (without skipping), and also to sing as the teacher calls for the sounds by their pitch names.]

XLIV. The pitch of a tone is represented to the eye by a line or space in what is called

THE STAFF.

The staff may have as many lines and spaces as there are different pitches of tones, each pitch having its own line or space to represent it (each line and space of the staff is called a degree). This would, however, make so many lines and spaces necessary, that it would be impossible to distinguish them quickly from another. To obviate this difficulty, three important plans have been made with regard to the staff.

XLV. The first is to print only five long lines, which, with the spaces between, and above and below them, afford the means for representing nearly all the pitches of the tones of vocal music; and when more degrees are wanted, add them by means of short lines. By this plan, any degree of the staff, whether made by a long line or space, or by a short or added one, is distinguished at a glance.

XLVI. Another plan about the staff is, to make the lines and spaces (degrees) of the staff stand for different pitches by means of characters called

CLEFS.

It may be said in passing that the use of clefs is an expedient to make the five long lines, with their spaces, represent as far as possible the pitches most commonly made use of, and so avoid, as much as possible, the added degrees.

XLVII. There are three clefs used in this book. The

TREBLE CLEF,

TREBLE CLEF.

Making the second line of the staff stand for the pitch G, and especially suited to ladies' voices; and the

TENOR CLEF,

TENOR CLEF.

Making the second line also stand for G, (or rather the third space for C, which, however, amounts to the same thing,) but suited to men's voices, and so to a pitch an octave lower than the treble. The other is called the

BASE CLEF,

BASE CLEF.

And makes the fourth line stand for F; also used for men's voices.

XLVIII. The third thing about the staff, is that each line and space may be made to stand for five different pitches, while using the same clef, by means of characters called respectively sharp, flat, double sharp and double flat. This expedient greatly diminishes the number of lines and spaces needed for the representation of the different pitches of tones, and greatly simplifies the appearance of the staff.

XLIX.

[It will now be readily seen, that the lines and spaces of the staff indicate the pitch of tones, but give no idea how long they should be, nor how loud or soft, and thus that the staff is only a melodic character—indicating nothing of rhythmics or dynamics.]

How is the length of a tone named? *How is the length of a tone represented?* *(By a note in both cases: we speak of singing quarter notes, and call the characters that stand for these sounds by the same name.)* *How are the pitches of tones named?* *By what are the pitches of tones represented?* *(Here the answers are different. Letters are the names of pitches, but the staff represents them to the eye. Some systems make the letters do this, but the staff is better, because it is pictorial.)* *How many long lines are there in the staff?* *How many spaces are there connected with these long lines?* *Would a staff be perfect that was written so near the top of a page or blackboard that there would be no space above, or so near the bottom that there would be no space below?* *Then do the space above or the space below belong to the staff, or are they added spaces?* *What is the first ADDED space?* *(Ans. That which is caused by the first added line).* *What other name has each line and space of the staff beside first line, first space, &c.?* *How many degrees are there in the staff, if you do not count the added degrees?* *What is the other name of the first degree?* *The second, &c.?* *(and so on through).* *How many clefs have we?* *What are their names?* *What does the treble clef indicate?* *What the tenor?* *What the base?* *In which department are we here studying?* *Is the staff a rhythmic, melodic, or dynamic character?* *In which department are clefs?*

CHAPTER V.

THE SCALE.

L. If you sing from the pitch C upwards, the eight tones next represented, you will observe a completeness in them that you have not experienced before.

La,   la,   la,   la,   la,   la,   la,   la.

[Male voices may sing from the treble clef, although it is not strictly correct to do so.]

LI. A series of tones having such a completeness is called a

SCALE.

A scale is a family of tones, eight in number, and as a family they have names that describe their family relations. These names are some of the names of numbers.

LII.

Scale names,	One,	two,	three,	four,	five,	six,	seven,	eight.
Pitch names,	C,	D,	E,	F,	G,	A,	B,	C.
Syllables,	Do,	re,	mi,	fa,	sol,	la,	si,	do.

[It is not necessary to use the tenor clef until the extension of the scale and the circumstances of the voices. The men at first may all sing from the base clef.]

LIII. You notice that the tone whose pitch is C (either the lower or the upper), has in this scale one peculiarity over all others, viz.: it is the most satisfactory as a resting or stopping place, or ending—indeed, a piece of music made of the tones of this scale could not sound finished or ended without it. This tone is called the key-note.

[In one of the old musical systems of Europe the syllables do, re, mi, &c., are used as the pitch names of tones; but when the names of letters are the pitch names, as in our country, the syllables are no more the names of tones than the words of a piece of poetry would be. They are used when there are no other words to the music, chiefly for the benefit of the pronunciation, enunciation and articulation.]

LIV. The difference of pitch between any two tones is called an

INTERVAL.

LV. There are two kinds of intervals, larger and smaller, in the scale. The larger are called

STEPS,

and the smaller,

HALF STEPS.

LVI. The intervals between three and four, and seven and eight, are half steps; all the others are steps

How many tones has the scale? What are their scale names? What is the pitch name of one? What is the pitch name of two? Of three? &c. It is common to drop this more correct phraseology (pitch name or name of the pitch) and say simply, the pitch; as for example, What is the pitch of one? What is the pitch of two? &c. What syllables are sometimes used in singing the scale, and tunes and exercises made from its tones? Are syllables the names of tones? What is one or eight of the tones of the scale called? What is the pitch of our key-note? Is the scale a rhythmic, melodic or dynamic character? What is the difference of pitch between any two tones called? How many intervals are there in the scale? How many kinds of intervals in the scale ?   What are they called ?   What is the name of the interval produced by one and two, or C and D ?   What by two and three, or D and E ?   Do intervals belong to Rhythmics, Melodics or Dynamics ?

CHAPTER VI.

VARIETIES OF MEASURE.

LVII. Thus far each part of a measure has been occupied by a quarter note, or its value. Any other kind of note may be taken for this purpose, and so we have

VARIETIES OF MEASURES.

[A tune will sound just the same whether represented with a quarter note (or its value), in each part of the measure, or a half or an eighth. In ordinary vocal music, varieties of measure are unnecessary; but, being in common use, we introduce them.]

LVIII. The different *varieties* of measures, as well as the different *kinds*, are indicated by figures in the form of fractions. The upper indicating the kind, and the lower the variety of measure.

LIX. There may be as many varieties of measures as there are kinds of notes. The following, however, are those only in common use.

LX.

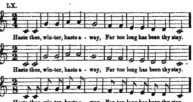

Haste thee, win-ter, haste a - way, Far too long has been thy stay.

Haste thee, win-ter, haste a - way, Far too long has been thy stay.

Haste thee, win-ter, haste a - way, Far too long has been thy stay.

[The above three examples all represent the first part of the same tune, and would be sung in the same time, and they show that notes do not represent positive, but only relative length.]

How are varieties of measures formed ?   What form do figures assume to indicate kinds and varieties of measures ?   Which figure indicates the kind of measure ?   Which the variety ?   Do notes represent positive or relative length ?   Do varieties of measure address the eye or ear ?   Do they belong to Rhythmics, Melodics, or Dynamics ?   What position should you take while singing ?   Should the breath be taken partly or fully ?   Should the tone be made with much breath or little ?   Should the throat assume a cramped and distorted, or a natural position ?   Should the mouth be too close, the tongue too much-raised, or drawn back into the throat, or any obstruction offered to the free giving out of the tone ?   What is the correct sound of the vowels called ?   (Ans. Good pronunciation).   What is the correct utterance of the consonants called ?   (Ans. Good enunciation).   What is the distinct and correct giving of each successive sound in singing called ?   (Ans. Good articulation).

[In a single tone, and in an exercise where there is no particular emotion to be expressed, singers will do well to aim simply at giving out or delivering the voice well, and attending to the other things of vocal culture and notation already mentioned, and not try to produce too much of an emotional tone ; that is, not try to make the voice sound large, deep, hollow, sad. &c., but reserve those qualities for words that call for them, and so avoid injury to the voice ; for, as the heart can not experience any strong emotion long at a time without injury to the health, so the tone that corresponds to it cannot be produced long at a time without injury to the voice.

This may be one of the reasons why so many voices give out while the health is in other respects good—such tones requiring distention and unusual positions of the throat, and can not safely be persisted in long at a time.]

CHAPTER VII.

EXTENDED SCALE AND CLASSIFICATION OF VOICES.

LXI. It is well for the pupils to understand the difference of pitch that exists between the adult male and female voice. To accomplish this, let all sing *eight* of the scale. They will really sing an octave apart.

the male voices thus :   and the female thus :

but most of the pupils will suppose that they are singing at the same pitch. There are various modes of making the right of this understood. One very good way is to have the female voices sustain eight, while the teacher (a man's voice) sings from his eight up to theirs. The blending at the last will show that he started an octave below, and came up to their pitch. Then have the men's voices sing their eight, and ask the females to give that exact pitch. Most of them will sing an octave too high at first ; but all can soon be brought to see that their one is .the same tone as to pitch, as the eight of the men's voices.

LXII. When men sing from the staff with the treble clef, they are not singing the exact pitch indicated, but what is called an eighth or octave below it. So, when women sing from the base clef, they sing an octave above *the real pitch indicated there.*

LXIII. Tones an octave apart have the same letters for pitch names, because there is such an agreement between them as to make them sound almost as if they were at the same pitch.

LXIV. The following example represents, as it were, a scale of two octaves in compass, and a larger staff made by putting the treble and base together (with one added line). Now, regard the male and female voices as one extended voice, and sing the following exercises, the former singing only on the base clef; and the latter on the treble (of course both singing on the added line).

LXV. The character at the beginning that connects these two staves is called a

BRACE.

A whole rest is also called a

MEASURE REST,

and is used to fill a measure in any kind of time

Sing we now the up-ward scale, Yes, sing we now the upward scale.

Down-ward, too, and do not fail, Yes, down-ward, too, we will not fail.

LXVI. Hitherto, the men have sung no higher than eight of their scale, or one of the scale represented on the treble staff. Let them now give that tone, and considering it one, go up the scale into the pitch of the treble staff, singing do, re, mi, &c.

LXVII. As it would not be convenient to represent the higher tones of men's voices by notes on the treble staff, we will represent them by added degrees on the base staff.

[It would be well here to explain with regard to registers, which subject will be found treated of in another place with other matters of the voice. It will, probably, be the case that some of the voices will have to change to the falsetto at two (D), certainly, some will change at three (E), and still more at four (F), leaving but few that can sing five (G), in the chest register. The pupils should be cautioned against straining their voices—encouraging them, however, to sing the high tones by using the falsetto, a certain amount of cultivation in that register being good for all, although only used in singing, by a certain kind of voice. When this is done, it should be said that those who can sing these higher tones (about F to G) without using the falsetto, may consider themselves *tenors*, or as possessing tenor voices, and in the following exercise may sing the upper part. The remainder of the men's voices may take the lower part, or, as it is commonly called, the base.]

LXVIII.

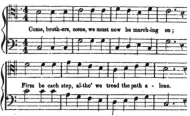

Come, broth-ers, come, we must now be march-ing on;

Firm be each step, al-tho' we tread the path a - lone

[It might be well to have each part sung alone at first, with the syllables, and perhaps with the words—observing as the first and most important thing, all that has before been taught with regard to the cultivation of the voice, and questioning upon the lessons as may be necessary.]

LXIX. It will now be seen why a tenor clef is used. In the follow-ing representation of the same song, it will be seen that it is easier for tenors to read the music, not only because they have a staff to themselv but because the use of added degrees is avoided.

Come, broth-ers, come, we must now be march-ing on;

Firm be each step, al-tho' we tread the path a - lone.

LXX. Let the female voices sing down into the pitches of the b: clef, commencing with what has been one to them, but now considering eight. Those who can sing these notes firmly, down as low as G, or five the base scale, can sing what is called ALTO, or SECOND.

LXXI. This part cannot be conveniently written on the base staff, the treble staff with added lines below, is used

Treble or Soprano.

Sis - ters, sis - ters, nev - er fear, Give the tones both firm and

clear, For the har - mo - ny pre - pare With the great-est   care.

[These parts would also be more easily sung if printed on separate staves.]

LXXII. Let the female voices now sing upward into the pitches represented by the third space, fourth line, fifth line, and space above in the treble
staff, to the syllables do, re, mi, &c. (they might, perhaps, finish the scale),
and then the men's voices go down into the pitches represented by the second space, second line, first space, and first line of the base staff, to the
syllables do, si, la, &c. (perhaps finishing the scale.) The voices may now
be named, according to compass, Soprano and Alto (1st and 2d Treble),
Tenor and Base. Those who cannot sing high enough to sing Tenor, are
advised to sing Base, even if they cannot sing very low, as it is more hurt-
ful to strain the voices upward than downward. The same about Soprano
and Alto.

LXXIII. The following example shows the way the four parts
are represented in our common vocal music, and also the compass of
each part.

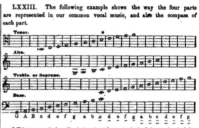

* This once marked small c, being about the center both of the vocal and of the
great or instrumental scale, is called the middle c.

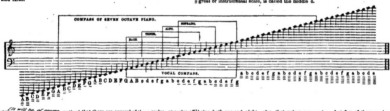

(It will be, of course, noticed that there are several of these scales, or series of being both one and eight; also, that voices can produce but few of these scales,
above (or below) each other, and joined together by each key-note many kinds of instruments going both higher and lower. As each series is named

as to pitch by the same letters (C, D, E, &c.), it is evident that they should have some mark to distinguish the particular series they belong to. This is done to the eye, by large and small letters and dashes, and to the ear by the use of the words large, small, once marked, twice marked, &c. For instance, the pitch indicated by the second space in the base is named small c ; the octave above that, (middle c) is named once marked small c ; the octave above that twice marked small c, and so on. The octave below the second space in the base is called large C ; the octave below that, once marked large C, and so on.]

[The foregoing diagram represents nearly the highest and lowest tones the ear can appreciate. As to the voice compass, some voices can go higher and some lower than the compass shown here, but those are about the tones used in ordinary vocal music.]

[It will be a pleasant exercise to start at middle C, and all go down as far as possible; then, starting at the same place, go up. Then, beginning as low as any of the voices can sound, go to the highest; then, if you have a piano or cabinet organ, let that begin at the lowest and go up, the voices joining when they can.]

How much difference of pitch is there between the adult male and female voice ? When men sing from the treble clef, how much lower do they sing than the pitch indicated ? Why do tones an octave apart have the same letters for a pitch name ? What is the character called that shows how many staves are to be used at once in a piece of music ? What peculiar use has the whole rest ? What are the higher male voices called ? What the lower ? What are the higher female voices called ? What the lower ? What clef is used to represent the exact pitch of tenor voices ? About how many of these eight-pitch scales, or octaves, are contained in the great scale of sounds ? How many are used in an ordinary piano ? How many in the vocal compass ? How many ordinarily in a single voice ? Since but seven letters are used as pitch names, how are the different octaves distinguished ? What is the once marked, small c called ?

CHAPTER VIII.

TRANSPOSITION.

LXXIV. The teacher will take the pitch G, and considering it in his own mind as eight of a new scale, sing down, thus :

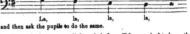

La,   la,   la,   la,

and then ask the pupils to do the same.

Those who have not studied music before will be surprised to learn, tl they are not singing F in their descent, but in its place another tone, a h step higher, named F sharp. When this is made manifest, and the sha explained, the teacher sings an exercise like the following, and asks if C now a good home, or resting place, or key-note.

[Observe, that the two preceding exercises are not written, but simply sung the teacher.]

LXXV. From this point it will not be difficult for the pupils to u derstand, that when F sharp is used instead of F, G becomes the key-nc of a new scale family—that A, instead of being six, is two ; B, three ; four ; D, five ; E, six ; F sharp, seven ; and G, eight, or one, again.

[As F sharp is much easier sung when in this way than when sung as a chr matic tone (sharp four in the key of C), nothing would here be said about the chr matic, nor would it be explained until after using all the intermediate tones, as th occur in the different major scales. It would be well, however, to *practise* the chr matic and minor scale as well as the major, by imitation, or rote, from a very ea period of the school.]

LXXVI. The term KEY is sometimes given to the tones of a scal The key of C, for example, consists of the tones A, B, C, D, E, F and (with this difference, between key and scale, that these tones in any orde either of succession or combination, are still the key of C, while only certain order of succession puts them into the form of the scale of C.

LXXVII. The key of G, consists of the tones A, B, C, D, E, F shar and G, in any order or combination they may have, while they form tl scale of G, only when they follow each other in intervals of seconds. W therefore, speak of a tune or piece of music as being in the *key* of G, or the *key* of C, rather than in the *scale* of G or C—the key-note, of course, giving the name to the key.

[It would be well now to practice in the key of G, by calling for various tones, the pupils applying "do" to one, "re" to two, "mi" to three, &c., bringing out the various intervals.

LXXVIII. It will be easily seen here; that the line and spaces of the staff that stand for the pitch whose name is F, are of no use as they are now, because we have no such pitch in the key of G. From this it is easy to show, that the character called a sharp modifies those lines and spaces, so that they no longer stand for F, but for F sharp.

[The attention of teachers is called to the fact that it is much easier to sing F sharp as one of the tones of a diatonic scale rather than as a chromatic tone; and much easier to represent it by modifying the line or space of the staff once for all throughout the entire tune, than to do so only for a measure or part of a measure, as is done by an accidental—consequently, that the key of G properly comes before the introduction of sharp four, or any other tone of the chromatic scale.]

G A B C D E F♯ G A B C D E F♯ G A B C D E F♯ G
1 2 3 4 5 6 7 1 2 3 4 5 6 7 1 2 3 4 5 6 7 8
Do re mi fa sol la si do re mi fa sol la si do re mi fa sol la si do

LXXIX. Since F sharp is a half step higher than F, it will be found that the steps and half steps occur in the same order in the scale of G that they do in the scale of C.

LXXX. The sharp, in the preceding lesson, not only modifies the degree of the staff on which it is placed, but every other degree named F; *and when so placed, is the* SIGNATURE *of the key of G. The absence of the sharp is the signature of the key of C.*

[If the pupils do not yet realise that they sing F sharp instead of F, it is easy to make it apparent by singing down from G, sometimes giving F, and sometimes F sharp.]

LXXXI. If you substitute C sharp for C, having all the other pitches the same as in the key of G, you will have a key or family of tones, of which the key-note is D.

LXXXII. The scale of D then consists of the tones D, E, F♯, G, A, B, C♯ and D, and will be just as easy to sing as the scale of C, because the steps and half steps occur in the same order.

[These tones, named with the word sharp, are no more difficult than the other tones when used in this way.]

LXXXIII. If you substitute G sharp for G, having all the other pitches as in the key of D, the result will be the key of A.

LXXXIV. The scale of A, consists of the tones A, B, C♯, D, E, F♯, G♯ and A.

LXXXV The key of E, consists of the tones A, B, C♯, D♯, E, F♯ and G♯. The scale of E consists of these tones in order from E to E inclusive.

LXXXVI. The key of B consists of the tones A♯, B, C♯, D♯, E, F♯ and G♯. The scale of B consists of these tones in order from B to B inclusive.

The key of F♯ sharp consists of the tones A♯, B, C♯, D♯, E♯, F♯ and G♯. The scale of F♯ is from F♯ to F♯ inclusive.

[It will be seen from the foregoing that a key consists of seven tones; but a scale, to be complete, must have eight.]

LXXXVII. These pitches, which have been named by the word sharp, are sometimes, for convenience, named in another manner; for instance, the pitch between A and B, which was before named A sharp is also sometimes called B flat, and a character called a flat is used to make the staff stand for this pitch when occasion requires.

LXXXVIII. The flat makes any degree of the staff on which it is placed stand for a pitch a half step lower than it does in the key of C.

LXXXIX. If you substitute B flat for B having all the other pitches, the same as in the key of C, the key of F will be the result. The scale of F consists of the tones F, G, A, B♭, C, D, E and F.

XC. If you substitute E flat for E, keeping the other pitches as in the key of F, the result will be the key of B flat. The scale of B flat consists of the tones B♭, C, D, E♭, F, G, A and B♭.

XCI. The scale of E flat consists of the tones E♭, F, G, A♭, B♭, C D and E♭. The key of E flat consists of these tones in any order.

XCII. The scale of A flat consists of the tones A♭, B♭, C, D♭, E♭, F, G and A♭.

XCIII. The scale of D flat, consists of the tones D♭, E♭, F, G♭, A♭, B♭, C and D♭.

XCIV. The scale of G flat consists of the tones G♭, A♭, B♭, C♭, D♭, E♭, F and G♭.

[These scales are easy to sing because the steps and half steps occur in the same order in each. In fact, the tones named by the words sharp and flat are used for the purpose of making this order of intervals, that the scales may be thus easy and natural; and these tones, when used in this way, are no more difficult to sing than any others, and are just as *natural*—using that word in its ordinary signification.]

[It will now be seen that a tone has two relations: one to the key in which it occurs, and another to the great scale of sounds. For instance: the tone C is *one* in one key; *two* in another; *four* in another; *three* in another; *six* in another, &c. It has, however, always its place or absolute pitch among all the sounds (irrespective of keys), that the ear can appreciate. So numerals are used as the names of *relative* pitch (scale relations), and letters as the names of absolute pitch.]

XCV. The following table shows the staves properly modified by sharps and flats to indicate the keys above mentioned.

What are the names of the pitches of the tones that make the key G ? (Begin the naming with A.) What pitch is used in the key of that is not found in the key of C ? What in the key of C, that is not the key of G ? What tones make the key of D ? What tones are h that are not in C ? What that are not in G ? (and so on of all scales.) How many tones does it take to make a key ? How many make a scale ? How does a key differ from a scale ? What is a k note ? How much higher is F sharp than F ? How much lower th G ? How much lower than G is G flat ? How much higher than is G flat ? Is the difference between F sharp and G flat a difference name or sound ? How does it affect a line or space of the staff to plac sharp upon it ? What is the effect of a flat ? Do sharps and flats

fect notes directly? (*Ans. No.*)   *What do they affect?* (*Ans. The staff only.*)   *Are the pitches in these scales that are named by the use of the word flat or sharp, any harder to sing than the others?*   *What is the pitch of one in the scale of C?*   *Of two?*   *What is the pitch of one in the key of G?*   *Of two?*   *Of three in the key of C?*   *Of three in the key of G?*   *Of three in E?*   *In A?*   *What is four in C?*   *In G?* (*and so on through all*).   *What is the name of the interval caused by one and two of any of these scales?*   *Two and three? Three and four?* (*and so on through all*).   *What is the signature of the key of G?*   (*Ans. One sharp*).   *What to the key of D?*   *What to A?   E?* (*and so on through all*).   *What syllable do you apply to one in any key?*   *Where do you get the pitch names of tones? Where the relative or scale names?*   *What is* RELATIVE *pitch?*   *What is* ABSOLUTE *pitch?*   *Are syllables the names of tones?*

CHAPTER IX.

MODULATION AND ACCIDENTALS.

XCVI. A piece of music begins and ends in the same key, but another key is often introduced during its progress.

XCVII. Going from one key to another during a piece of music is called

MODULATION.

Modulation is, therefore, indicated by changing the signification of the lines or spaces of the staff somewhere *in the tune*, instead of at the beginning. The characters that do this are called

ACCIDENTALS,

when so used.

XCVIII. *It's line or space* already modified by a sharp, or a flat, is to be restored to its original signification, a character called a *natural* (♮), is made use of. Sharps, flats and naturals, when used as signatures, affect the lines or spaces upon which they are placed, *throughout the tune*, or until contradicted by another signature, or by accidentals; whereas, the same characters when used as accidentals, only affect the line or space upon which they are placed *to the end of the measure* in which they occur. This rule has but one exception, viz.: when the last note of the measure is on the degree of the staff affected by the accidental, and the first note of the next measure is on the same degree, the effect of the accidental continues through that measure also, thus making it possible to continue the effect of an accidental through many measures.

XCIX. The effect of an accidental may at any time be done away by another accidental.

C. In the following tune, the introduction of the tones F sharp instead of F, brings in the key of G, which, in this case, continues through the second line.

The natural in the third line stops the power of the sharp (which otherwise would continue through the measure), and makes that space of the staff stand for F again. The B flat brings in the key of F, but the effect of the accidental does not continue beyond the measure in which it occurs.

1. Breath-ing so soft-ly a - long the gay mead, The spring time is
2. Flow'r-ets a-wake in the sweet ver-nal air, And fling their new

com - ing a - - gain ;   Laugh-ing rills dance on .the
o - dors *a - - round ;   Song birds re-turn - ing from

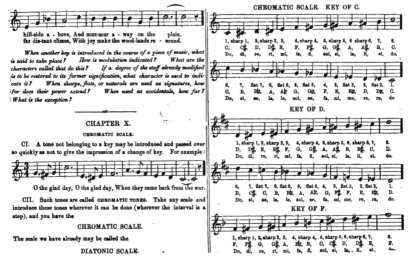

hill-side a - bove, And mur-mur a - way on the plain.
far dis-tant climes, With joy make the wood-lands re - sound.

When another key is introduced in the course of a piece of music, what is said to take place? How is modulation indicated? What are the characters called that do this? If a degree of the staff already modified is to be restored to its former signification, what character is used to indicate it? When sharps, flats, or naturals are used as signatures, how far does their power extend? When used as accidentals, how far? What is the exception?

CHAPTER X.

CHROMATIC SCALE.

CI. A tone not belonging to a key may be introduced and passed over so quickly as not to give the impression of a change of key. For example:

O the glad day, O the glad day, When they came back from the war.

CII. Such tones are called CHROMATIC TONES. Take any scale and introduce these tones wherever it can be done (wherever the interval is a step), and you have the

CHROMATIC SCALE.

The scale we have already may be called the

DIATONIC SCALE.

CHROMATIC SCALE. KEY OF C.

1, sharp 1, 2, sharp 2, 3, 4, sharp 4, 5, sharp 5, 6 sharp 6, 7, 8.
C, C♯, D, D♯, E, F, F♯, G, G♯, A, A♯, B,, C.
Do, di, re, ri, mi, fa, fi, sol, si, la, li, si, do.

8, 7, flat 7, 6, flat 6, 5, flat 5, 4, 8, flat 3, 3, flat 2, 1.
C, B, B♭, A, A♭, G, G♭, F, E, E♭, D, D♭, C.
Do, si, se, la, le, sol, se, fa, mi, me, re, ra, do

KEY OF D.

1, sharp 1, 2, sharp 2, 3, 4, sharp 4, 5, sharp 5, 6, sharp 6, 7, 8.
D, D♯, E, E♯, F, G, G♯, A, A♯, B, B♯, C, D.
Do, di, re, ri, mi, fa, fi, sol, si, la, li, si, do.

8, 7, flat 7, 6, flat 6, 5, flat 5, 4, 3, flat 3, 2, flat 2, 1.
D, C♯, C, B, B♭, A, A♭, G, G♯, F, E, E♭, D.
Do, si, se, la, le, sol, se, fa, mi, me, re, ra, do.

KEY OF F.

1, sharp 1, 2, sharp 2, 3, 4, sharp 4, 5, sharp 5, 6, sharp 6, 7, 8.
F, F♯, G, G♯, A, B♭, B, C, C♯, D, D♯, E, F.
Do, di, re, ri, mi, fa, fi, sol, si, la, li, si, do.

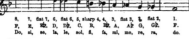

8,	7,	flat 7,	6,	flat 6,	5,	sharp 4,	4,	3,	flat 3,	2,	flat 2,	1.
F,	E,	E♭,	D,	D♭,	C,	B,	B♭,	A,	A♭,	G,	G♭,	F.
Do,	si,	se,	la,	le,	sol,	fi,	fa,	mi,	me,	re,	ra,	do.

[Since sharps, flats and naturals do not affect notes, but degrees of the staff, chromatic tones cannot be indicated in a signature.]

When a tone not belonging to a key is passed over so quickly as not to change the key, what is it called ?   How is the chromatic scale formed ? How many tones has the chromatic scale ?   What are their scale names ? What their pitch names ?   What syllables are affixed to them ?   What syllables are applied to them ?   What kind of interval occurs in the chromatic scale ?

CHAPTER XI.

THE MINOR SCALE.

CIII. Take away five in either of the keys we have been using, and substitute a tone a half step higher, and a great change will be made; not only another key will be the result, but it will be a key of a different kind, more sad and mournful. Take out G from the tones that make the key of C, for example, and put in its place G sharp, and you have a key of this kind. It is called a *minor key.*

CIV. The keys we have been using are called *major keys.* (There are no chromatic keys—chromatic tones may come into major and minor keys).

CV. Here is a tune in this key that is made of the tones A, B, C, D, E, F, and G sharp. Try to tell by the sound what the key-note is.

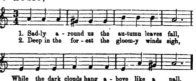

1. Sad-ly   a - round us   the   au-tumn leaves   fall,
2. Deep in the   for - est   the   gloom-y winds   sigh,

While   the dark clouds hang   a - bove   like   a   pall.
Bird songs and flow - ers   no   long - er   are   nigh.

[The G sharp, which is one of the tones of this key, is represented by an accidental, and not in the signature. One reason for this is, that relative keys may have the same signature ; another is, that another kind of minor scale has G in it as well as G sharp.]

CVI. The key-note here is A.

CVII. The key of A minor is said to be the relative minor to the key of C major.

CVIII. Every major key has its relative minor, and every minor its relative major.

CIX. That which is six in a major key is one in its relative minor, and that which is three in a minor key is one in its relative major

CX.   SCALE OF A MINOR.

1,	2,	3,	4,	5,	6,	7,	8,	8,	7,	6,	5,	4,	3,	2,	1.
A,	B,	C,	D,	E,	F,	G♯,	A,	A,	G♯,	F,	E,	D,	C,	B,	A.
La,	si,	do,	re,	mi,	fa,	si,	la,	la,	si,	fa,	mi,	re,	do,	si,	la.

CXI. A degree of the staff that is already modified by a sharp, can be made to stand for a pitch still half a step higher by placing upon it a character called a double sharp (×), and a character called a double flat (♭♭), makes a degree of the staff already affected by a flat, stand for a pitch still a half step lower

[It will be remembered that keys having the same signature are said to be rela-tive keys.]

CXII. The following table shows the signatures and key-notes of the minor keys.

[There are several kinds of minor scales. The one used here is generally con-sidered the best. It is called the harmonic minor scale.]

How is the minor key made from any major key ?   What tones make the key of A minor ?   What the key of E minor ? (and so on through the keys).   What is the relative minor to C major ?   What is the relative major to A minor ?   What is the relative minor to G major ?   What the relative major to E minor ? (and so on through the keys).

CHAPTER XII.

DYNAMICS.

CXIII. If you sing a sound with medium strength, it is said to be mezzo (pronounced metzo), and is indicated by this word or its abbrevia-tion.

CXIV. The following table gives the names and abbreviations of the different dynamic degrees, with their meanings.

Pianissimo (pp), very soft.
Piano (p), soft.
Mezzo piano (m p), between medium and soft.
Mezzo (m), medium.
Mezzo forte (mf), between medium and loud.
Forte (f), loud.
Fortissimo (ff), very loud.

CXV. The following table shows other dynamic names and charac-ters, which are, however, made known under the head of EXPRESSION.

Organ tone ⸺, a tone commenced, continued and ended with the same strength.

Crescendo (cres. or ◁), commencing soft, and gradually in-creasing.

Diminuendo (dim or >—), commencing loud, and gradually diminishing.

Swell (<———>), a union of the crescendo and diminuendo.

Pressure tone (<), a sudden crescendo.

Forzando (>), a sudden diminuendo

What is the name in music for a very soft tone ? What is its abbreviation ? What is the musical name of a soft tone ? What is its abbreviation ? (and so on through the table). What is an organ tone ? What is a crescendo ? (and so on.)

CHAPTER XIII.

MISCELLANEOUS.

CXVI. Where different tones are closely connected, they are said to be LEGATO. Such a style is indicated by a curve (———), over or under the notes.

CXVII. When such a line is placed over or under two notes on the same degree of the staff, it makes them stand for one sound, and is then called a tie.

CXVIII. When tones are made that are disconnected—as it were pointed—they are said to be STACCATO. This style of performance is indicated by characters like the following, one over each note (׀ ׀ ׀ ׀).

CXIX. Half way between *legato* and *staccato*, is MARCATO, indicated by a dot over each note.

CXX. A PAUSE (⌒), placed over or under a note, indicates that the *tones to be sung* should be prolonged beyond the tone usually indicated by

CXXI. Dots placed before a bar, signify REPEAT. Their influence extends back to the beginning of the piece, or to a double bar, or to dots placed across the staff.

CXXII. DA CAPO, or D. C., signifies go back to the beginning, and close at the word FINE. DAL SEGNO, or D. S., signifies go back to the sign 𝄋.

CHAPTER XIV.

THE VOICE.

CXXIII. It may be well to present here, in a condensed form, those points in vocal culture which, in addition to what have been mentioned, are useful for singers to know, and as occasion may require, to practice.

The organs of the voice may be enumerated and defined as follows :

THE LUNGS.—Something like sponges that may be distended or compressed at pleasure, by filling their cells with air, and breathing it out again.

THE ABDOMINAL and INTERCOSTAL MUSCLES, under and at the sides of the lungs, that do the work of distending and compressing them.

The WINDPIPE or TRACHEA that goes from the lungs to

The LARYNX (Adam's apple), in which are

The VOCAL CHORDS; which consist of two muscles, something like lips, that when brought together, and the air forced between them, vibrate and produce the voice. The opening caused by these muscles is called

The GLOTTIS, which may be called the mouth of the windpipe. If the tone could be heard just as it comes from the glottis, without a place to resound in, it would probably be anything but agreeable; but it passes into

The PHARYNX, a flexible cavity, which may be seen just above the roots of the tongue, and there receives to a great degree its musical quality, and then to the mouth, where it may be formed into words.

BREATHING.

The breath should be taken by spreading the ribs apart and raising them upward, at the same time drawing in at the waist. When the lungs are thus filled, they seem to press upward, and to be fullest and most distended at the top, which is the best possible position for managing the breath, and for giving the singer confidence that it will not give out. This latter condition is, however, not fully attained unless the use of the breath in singing be in the right way, and that includes the two following important things, viz.: making use of as little breath as possible, and holding the abdominal muscles firmly in their *drawn in* position. In words, the breath should generally be taken only when marks of pronunciation or rhetorical pauses would be proper. Taking the breath in the syllables of a word, or after unaccented words, should be avoided.

DELIVERY OF THE VOICE.

A good delivery of the voice depends upon adjusting the vocal organs for each word or vowel sound, so that there shall be no unnecessary obstruction by lips, teeth, tongue, or contraction of the throat. Some of the words and sounds of our language are much better for forming and delivering the tone than others; still, the words should not be sacrificed to the sound, although they may sometimes render a good delivery difficult. Common faults in this matter are closing the lips or teeth too much, raising the tongue or drawing it back into the throat, and contracting the throat.

PRONUNCIATION AND ENUNCIATION.

Good pronunciation depends upon forming and giving the vowel sounds correctly, and good enunciation upon the distinct utterance of the consonants. As more strength in the various muscles of articulation is required for singing than for ordinary speaking, frequent practice of the elements alone, separated from words, is very beneficial.

VOCAL ELEMENTS.

Give each vowel its exact sound, and see that the tones are well and delivered. Do not distend the pharynx, or in any way try to m voice *emotional*, for there is here no emotion to be expressed. Si that the tones are given without obstruction from lips, tongue or te the lungs are well and rightly filled, and the breath properly used, the vowel sounds are pure and exact. Sing two or more measu breath, if you can, but do not exhaust the lungs. Connect the fou well together.

CONSONANT ELEMENTS.

Observe that you are to give the sounds that these letters stand the language, and not the names of the letters themselves. For instance, l indicates the first of the two elements that make the word " la," which is given while the end of the tongue is held against the roof of the mouth just back of the front teeth—the sound, of which m is the sound, with the mouth closed ; n as in no, v as in vow, th as in thou, d as in do, b as in bow, g as in go, r as in row, which should be rolled or trilled, not much. but enough to give force and distinctness.

1.	l	l	l	l	l	l	l	l	l	l	l	l	l	l	l
2.	m	m	m	m	m	m	m	m	m	m	m	m	m	m	m
3.	n	n	n	n	n	n	n	n	n	n	n	n	n	n	n
4.	v	v	v	v	v	v	v	v	v	v	v	v	v	v	v
5.	th	th	th	th	th	th	th	th	th	th	th	th	th	th	th
6.	d	d	d	d	d	d	d	d	d	d	d	d	d	d	d
7.	b	b	b	b	b	b	b	b	b	b	b	b	b	b	b
8.	g	g	g	g	g	g	g	g	g	g	g	g	g	g	g
9.	r	r	r	r	r	r	r	r	r	r	r	r	r	r	r

REGISTERS

All singers can produce series of different kinds of tones, technically called Registers; and, if they sing through the whole extent of the voice, cannot avoid making them. For example, a male voice beginning with a low tone cannot ascend to his highest without breaking more or less distinctly into a more feminine and fluty kind of tone, usually known as falsetto. It is a singular fact, that all voices—both of men and women—make the change of register in about the same place. All go from their lowest tone up to about middle C (say from middle C to the G next above), with a firm and masculine kind of voice, called the lower or chest register, then a *smooth or and* more fluty kind of voice begins, and continues to about one octave above middle C; and this is called in women's voices the medium regis-

ter, and in men's voices the falsetto. At about this point another change takes place, and the voice again assumes a firmer and more ringing quality, which continues upward through the remainder of its compass. This is called in women's voices the upper register, but in men's voices not named, as it almost never used. Indeed, men use the second register, or falsetto, but little, and many voices not at all—the lowest, or chest register being that which includes almost all their available tones. Some female voices make excellent use of the few tones of the chest register that are allotted to the sex, while others use it too much and too high ; and still others, who, from natural organism or neglect, have so little strength in its tones, that they make but little use of it. The medium and upper registers are, consequently, the most important to the female voice. It is not desirable that the break from one register to the other should be removed, for by it beautiful effects are sometimes produced. The great work is equalising these registers, and it is accomplished by practicing on the lower tones of the medium register, until they become more firm, like those of the lower, and modifying the upper tones of the lower register, until they come nearer the quality of the medium. Those who sing alto are often tempted to carry the chest register too high, not only producing, in doing so, a harsh, masculine tone, but weakening the lower part of the medium register, and injuring, if not destroying, the symmetry that should exist in every cultivated voice. The practice of the registers is excellent for every voice, if they are kept in their proper limits. No voice is injured by singing where it produces the tone easily ; but the organs of the voice, like other parts of the body, may be strained and overworked, and as it were sprained and even broken.

QUALITIES OF TONE.

All persons who have the capacity to experience the different kinds or grades of joy and sorrow, fear, reverence, awe, &c., have the organs and powers for giving them exact and true expression, and the different sounds of the notice that are used for this purpose are technically called qualities of tone. The pharynx is the organ by which the qualities of tones are principally made, and when guided by right understanding of this subject, and accustomed to be shaped into the right form to express the emotions of the singer, becomes wonderfully sensitive to every shade of feeling. Some singers seem to adjust the pharynx to produce one quality of tone, and this tone they never vary except to make it louder and softer. If a base, he distends the pharynx, perhaps, so that he may get the large or deep quality that he delights in ; and this prevails, whatever may be the subject of his song. Such a person seems always to be thinking of his voice, instead of what he is singing about, and, of course, never gives a true expression, excepting to words that belong to that quality. Another has a preference for a different quality ; but his performance is liable to the same objection, if he does not change according to the emotion to be expressed.

The following table, from Palmer's "Rudimental Class Teaching," shows at a glance all the sounds of our language.

A has four sounds—ale, arm, all, at.
B has one sound—babble.
C has four sounds—city, come, discern, ocean.
D has two sounds—deed, effaced.
E has two sounds—eel, ell.
F has two sounds—fly, of.
G has three sounds—gem, goes, mirage (merush).
H has one sound—high.
I has two sounds—isle, ill.
J has one sound—June.
K has one sound—kirk.
L has one sound—listlessly.
M has one sound—mum.
N has two sounds—moon, bank.
O has three sounds—ode, moon, box.
P has one sound—peep.
Q has one sound—queen.

R has two sounds—farm, bright.
S has four sounds—so, as, sure, treasure.
T has two sounds—title, portion.
U has three sounds—mule, up, full.
V has one sound—vivid.
W has two sounds—way-ward, pow-wow.
X has three sounds—ex, exist, Xerxes.
Y has three sounds—yet, rhyme, hymn.
Z has two sounds—fizzle, azure.
Ch has three sounds—cheek, chagrin, choir.
Gh has three sounds—cough, aghast, furlough.
Ph has one sound—nephew.
Th has two sounds—thin, then.
Wh has one sound—when.
Oi has one sound—oil.
Ou has two sounds—found, soup.

The foregoing subjects may be taken up at any time in the progress of a class, and practiced upon more or less, according to circumstances. The opening of each lesson is a good time to do this ; and a good way is, to have the teacher sing as he wishes the pupils to sing, and have them imitate. The exercise should follow from teacher to pupil without loss of time, and with constant variety. He can in this way give out just such tones and vowel sounds and words as are most needed, and in the way they should

be done, and make the work more lively and interesting than by using either book or blackboard ; or, he can call for tones of the scale (after they have learned the scale), making a point of whatever he is practicing.

As before intimated, it would be well to practice the major, minor and chromatic scales by rote from an early period. Such practice is not only of great importance in the real work of learning to sing, and of training the musical perceptions, voice and taste, but may be made very interesting. The teacher sings such a tone, or phrase, or scale, or part of a scale, as he wishes the class to learn, and they give it after him—first one, then the other (teacher and class), in perfect time—the teacher adapting his examples to their capacity and their needs, and drawing, perhaps, his examples and illustrations from the surrounding circumstances. This course keeps the work fresh and full of life, the teacher making constant variety in his examples, and the class watching with interest the new things that the teacher brings out, and always keeping themselves ready to "follow the leader."

This plan of alternate singing-between teacher and pupils is excellent for improvement in all the points of vocal culture : and since music is so eminently an imitative art, this is a legitimate and orderly way of making attainment in it.

It is quite an art to do this kind of work, for it requires not only knowledge and musical skill, but fertility of invention, and great readiness and aptness in "turning things to account" However, "practice makes perfect," in this as in other things, and all who will, may acquire it in some degree.

It is an excellent plan to spend the first half hour of each lesson in this "*viva voce*" (living voice) teaching and practice, and preparation for it on the part of the teacher will be time well spent. The major, minor and chromatic scales, the elements of language, the different qualities of tone, exercises for execution and expression, and many other things in music, are, doubtless, best learned in this way

CHAPTER XV.

ELEMENTARY HARMONY.

CXIV. We have called the scale a family of tones, with C for the principal one, or, as it were, the head of the family. Each tone of the scale may in turn be the principal of another kind of family, called a chord. A chord consists of three or more tones of different pitches heard together.

The chord family is different from the scale family, inasmuch as it consists of tones heard together, while the scale consists of tones heard one after another, or, the scale consists of seconds *succeeding* each other, while the chord consists of different intervals produced *simultaneously.*

When we hear a choir sing, or a band play, or a piano or an organ, the music consists mostly of a succession of chords. The one most used is called the common chord.

The common chord is made by taking any tone, and giving it, with its third and fifth, or, in other words, by considering any tone of the scale *one,* and finding from it, *three and five,* and then combining them together. Let us take C as *one,* all singing it to "la;" now sing *three* from it, or a third (remember that intervals are always reckoned upward, unless otherwise especially directed); now *five* from it, or a fifth. Now choose which you please, the principal tone, or its third or fifth, and give them all together. In doing this, you are producing the common chord of C.

The female voices are singing what would be noted thus :

The male voices what would be noted thus :

If both are right; and were one, three and five to be given in a still *v scale, or in a lower* one, they would be right also. Any possible combination of the tones C, E and G, or all the tones named with these letters, make only the common chord of C.

In the study of chords every tone and its octave are regarded as the same ; for example, in the chord of C, every C is regarded as one, or eight ; every E, three ; and every G, five—so that any E is the third in the chord of C, and any G the fifth. According to this, there are but three different tones in the common chord, although by doubling them or adding their octaves, you may increase the number.

Vocal music is mostly written in four parts ; therefore, to give each part a tone, one of the tones of the common chord must be doubled, or its octave taken. We have *one, three, five,* and *one* or *eight ;* or, we may have *one, three, five* and *five* (at the same pitch, or an octave above or below) ; or, we may double the third, although that is avoided as much as possible.

Bases sing one, altos *three,* tenors *five,* and sopranos *eight.* This would be represented thus :

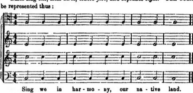

Sing we   in   har - mo - ny,   our   na - tive land.

If any possible combination of the tones C, E and G will make the common chord of C, it follows that the common chord of C may have many forms. In the following lesson, some of the forms are given that it may have within the vocal compass. Observe that all the tones of this lesson are in the common chord of C. Please notice while you sing, whether you are giving the principal tone of the chord, or its third or fifth.

Let us now sing a song in which we shall have alternately the common chord of C, and the common chord of G, or the chord formed on *one* of the scale and chord formed on *five*. It will be a very good plan to name the chords before singing. As the tone G belongs to both chords, when you see that note in the part you sing, you will have to notice the other parts before you can tell which chord it belongs to.

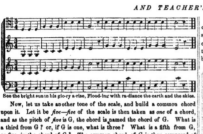

See the bright sun in his glo-ry a-rise, Flood-ing with ra-diance the earth and the skies.

Now, let us take another tone of the scale, and build a common chord upon it. Let it be *five—five* of the scale is then taken as *one* of a chord, and as the pitch of *five* is G, the chord is named the chord of G. What is a third from G? or, if G is one, what is *three?* What is a fifth from G, or five, in the chord of G? The common chord of G is then composed of the tones G, B and D. All sing these tones, giving them one after the other; then, choosing which you please, sing them all together. You observe that the lesson consists of different forms of but one chord, that which is formed on G, or five of the scale. It will be an excellent plan to name before singing, the tones each part has (first, third, fifth, or one three, five.)

Up-ward, still up-ward, the sun mounts on high, In the deep blue of the clear sum-mer sky.

Wel-come, wel-come, hour of song, Pleas-ant is thy sway— } At thy pres-ence, pure and bright, E - vil flies a - way. } Rest thee here, sweet hour of song.

Fold thy sil-ver wing; And with my heart, and hand and voice, Glad thy praise I'll sing.

Let us now form a chord on *four* of the scale. All sing *four*, now a third above it, now a fifth. We see that taking *four* of the scale as *one* of the chord, *one*, *three* and *five* gives us F, A and C, or the common chord of

F. Now practice different forms of this chord in lessons like the preceding. Notice the fact that the tone C belongs not only to the chord of C, but to the chord of F (just as G belongs both to the chord of C and the chord of G). Let the pupils name the chords in the following lesson, which consists of the three chords introduced—the chord on *one* of the scale, the chord on *five* of the scale, and the chord on *four*.

O - ver the mead-ows so pearl - y,   Soft-ly   the breez-es   stray,

Bear-ing the song of the wild-bird, Far to the wood-lands a - way.

We could form a common chord on two of the scale, on three, and on six and seven; but the common chords of those tones sound very differently from those that we have; and as they are but little used, we will not introduce them here.

The key-note, in music is sometimes called the Tonic, and the chord founded upon it the Tonic chord. *Five* of the scale is sometimes called the Dominant, and *four* the Subdominant; and the chords founded upon them are often called the Dominant and the Subdominant chords.

All sing the tonic chord. Take any tone you please; now again, singing the words "Hail! happy day." Sing the subdominant chord to the same words, now the dominant, and after that the tonic to end with.

You will find that it will not be satisfactory to close a piece of music on any other chord than the tonic chord. What tone of the scale is the tonic chord founded on? What the dominant? What the subdominant?

Bases sing one of the dominant chord, tenors three, and altos five (G, B, D).

We will now make a new chord, by having the soprano add F, or *seven*, to this common chord. This makes what is called the chord of the seventh, and would be represented thus:

You perceive that the chord of the seventh, unlike the common chord, has four different tones—the tone on which it is founded, and its third, fifth and seventh; or, it is like the common chord, only with a seven added instead of eight. The chord of the seventh does not sound well, founded upon the tonic or subdominant, so we shall use it for the present only on the dominant. The chord of the seventh may have more forms than the common chord, because it has more tones.

In the following lesson, the tonic chord is occasionally introduced, because it is not pleasant to stay too long at a time upon the chord of the seventh. It is, of course, understood that any possible combination of the tones G, B, D and F, is only the chord of the seventh of G.

which we cannot now explain. Before singing the following lesson, na each chord, and while singing it, try to notice at each syllable, whether are singing *one, three, five* or *seven* of a chord.

Now gent-ly flows the song, Now firm-er and more strong; Now loud-er still, with right good will, The joy-ful notes pro-long.

1. Spring time is com-ing, and we will be mer-ry, Tra, la, la, la, la, la,
2. While we are sing ing, the song-birds are call-ing, Tra, la, la, la, la, la, la, la.

Good bye, De-cem-ber and cold Jan-u-a-ry, Tra, la, la, la, la, la, la,
Sweet on the ear is their mel-o-dy fall-ing, Tra, la, la, la, la, la, la, la.

It will be seen that the common chord is sometimes used without a fifth, and the chord of the seventh sometimes without a fifth, and sometimes without a third. This is done partly because it would not always sound well, and would be difficult to have a part (soprano, alto, tenor or base), jump about so as to make the chord full, and partly for other reasons

It may be well here to state, that all the different forms of a cho that can be made, while keeping the base *one*, are said to be differences of *po tions*, and that the differences made by changing the base are called *inversin* When the base takes *three*, the chord is said to be in its *first inversio* and when the base takes five, it is said to be in its *second* inversion. Since the chord of the seventh has one more tone than the common chord, it can have one more inversion. So, seven in the base in the chord of the seventh makes the *third* inversion. When the base is one, the chord is said to be *direct.*

POSITIONS OF THE COMMON CHORD.

INVERSIONS OF THE COMMON CHORD.

INVERSIONS OF THE CHORD OF THE SEVENTH.

Now form the common chord on the tonic in the key of G. Now on the subdominant. Now on the dominant. Now tonic to close with. This would be illustrated thus, (such a succession of chords is called a cadence)

You might chant to each chord such a phrase as "Hail! happy day," or a line of poetry, and so sing a four line verse to the cadence. The following exercise on the tonic, sub-dominant, dominant and tonic will illustrate.

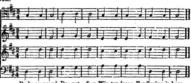

Buds ap-pear! Do not fear Win-ter drear, For Spring is here.

It would be an excellent plan to form and practice in this way the tonic, subdominant and dominant chords in each key After this, it would be well to analyze the chords in the lessons of the elementary course, particularly the one which goes through all the keys on page 79.

We have here but entered on the subject of harmony. Many chords are used in this book that we have not here spoken of. But what has been done will point out the way in which this important subject should be studied.

ELEMENTARY COURSE.

When the Scale, Staff, Quarter Notes and Clef have been introduced, these lessons may be commenced. As men are often called upon to sing from the treble staff, and women often find it desirable to read from the base, exercises for all are written on both. Introduce the new subjects mentioned over each lesson before practicing it.

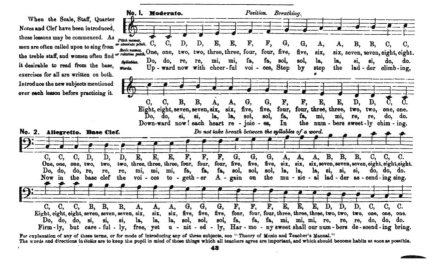

No. 1. Moderato.   *Position. Breathing.*

Pitch names, or absolute pitch. C, C, D, D, E, E, F, F, G, G, A, A, B, B, C, C.
Tonic names, or relative pitch.
Syllables. Do, do, re, re, mi, mi, fa, fa, sol, sol, la, la, si, si, do, do.
One, one, two, two, three, three, four, four, five, five, six, six, seven, seven, eight, eight.
Words. Up - ward now with cheer - ful voi - ces, Step by step the lad - der climb - ing,

C, C, B, B, A, A, G, G, F, F, E, E, D, D, C, C.
Eight, eight, seven, seven, six, six, five, five, four, four, three, three, two, two, one, one.
Do, do, si, si, la, la, sol, sol, fa, fa, mi, mi, re, re, do, do.
Down - ward now! each heart re - joic - es, In the num - bers sweet - ly chim - ing.

No. 2. Allegretto. Base Clef.   *Do not take breath between the syllables of a word.*

C, C, C, D, D, D, E, E, E, F, F, F, G, G, G, A, A, A, B, B, B, C, C, C.
One, one, one, two, two, two, three, three, three, four, four, four, five, five, five, six, six, six, seven, seven, seven, eight, eight, eight.
Do, do, do, re, re, re, mi, mi, mi, fa, fa, fa, sol, sol, sol, la, la, la, si, si, si, do, do, do.
Now in the base clef the voi - ces to - geth - er A - gain on the mu - sic - al lad - der as - cend - ing sing.

C, C, C, B, B, B, A, A, A, G, G, G, F, F, F, E, E, E, D, D, D, C, C, C.
Eight, eight, eight, seven, seven, seven, six, six, six, five, five, five, four, four, four, three, three, three, two, two, two, one, one, one.
Do, do, do, si, si, si, la, la, la, sol, sol, sol, fa, fa, fa, mi, mi, mi, re, re, re, do, do, do.
Firm - ly, but care - ful - ly, free, yet u - nit - ed - ly, Har - mo - ny sweet shall our num - bers de - scend - ing bring.

For explanation of any of these terms, or for mode of introducing any of these subjects, see "Theory of Music and Teacher's Manual."
The words and directions in *italics* are to keep the pupil in mind of those things which all teachers agree are important, and which should become habits as soon as possible.

43

BUILDING THE SCALE.

No. 3. Double Measure. Figures. Half Note. Bar. Double Bar.

[*This page is inserted for those who desire a more gradual development of the scale.*]

No. 4. Beating Time. Commencing on Five.
Moderate. *Give out the tone without obstruction from tongue, teeth or lips.*

Down, up, down up, Beat and sing, Re, mi, fa, sol, la, si, do, Give the hands a grace-ful swing, All to-geth-er as we go.

No. 5. Commencing on Three. Skips. One, Three, Five and Eight.
Moderate. *Fill the lungs at each inspiration.*

Three, two, one, three, two, one, Now the skips our voi-ces try, Mi, re, do, mi, re, do, But we'll con-quer by and by.

No. 6. Mezzo. Forte.
Allegretto. *Give out the consonants distinctly.*

When you see the let-ter M, Mez-zo you must sing, sir, But when F is writ-ten down, Make the mu-sic ring, sir.

No. 7. Piano.
Andantine. *Give the right sound to the vowels.*

Soft-ly sing, soft-ly sing, Let the tones be soft and low, When-e'er you see the let-ter P, For it means sing soft, you know.

No. 8.
Moderate. *Position. Breathing. Enunciation. Pronunciation.*

Mez-zo, for-te and pi-a-no, Me-dium, loud and gen-tle, Give them out in or-der fair, With-out a frown or wrin-kle

No. 9. Triple Measure. Dotted Half Notes.
Moderate.

Down, left, up down, left, up, three, three, three, four, G, G, G, la, la, la, B, B, B, do, down, left, up, sol, four, three, two, do.
Now let the tones of the new meas-ure ring, For you will find it a ver-y good thing; ver-y good thing; ver-y good thing.

No. 10. Crescendo, Fortissimo.
Allegro.

1. Haste ye a - way! haste ye a - way! For it is com - ing, 'tis com - ing, 'tis com - ing, O
2. Haste to the wild, maid - en and child; Where is the drum - ming, the chirp and the hum - ming, O

haste ye ..a - way, Haste ye a - way, For it is com - ing, the beau - ti - ful day, beau - ti - ful day.
there Spring hath smil'd, Haste to the wild, Spring time is com - ing, sweet maid - en and child, maid - en and child.

No. 11. Diminuendo. Crescendo.
Andante.

1. Slow-ly sound-ing a - long the dell, Hear the tones of the ev'n-ing bell, Rest from la-bor its num-bers tell, Its plain-tive num-bers tell.
2. Soft - ly trill-ing a child-ish lay, Birds and bees 'mid the blos-soms gay, These we heard when the morn was grey, A sim-ple bird-like lay:

No. 12. Quadruple Measure. Whole Note.
Moderate.

Down, left, right, up, down, left, right, up, three, three, three, three, four, G, G, G, G, la, la, la, la, down, left, right, up, eight.
1. E - ven meas-ure, what a pleas-ure, 'Tis the time to keep; High-er mounting, to the count-ing, As we on-ward sweep.
2. Roll for - ev - er, rap - id riv - er, Thine a sweet-er song. On thy bo - som hill - side blos - som Sea-ward floats a - long.

No. 13.   *Position. Breathing. Enunciation. Pronunciation. Articulation. Throat and mouth opened naturally.*
Allegretto.

1. Bird - ie sweet, Bird - ie sweet, Where may you be go - ing? From the North, Has-ten South, Fear-ful winds are blow - ing.
2. Bird - ie sweet, Bird - ie sweet, When you are re - turn - ing, Come to me, Let me see, What new songs you're learn-ing.

No. 14. Sextuple Measure. Dotted Whole Note.

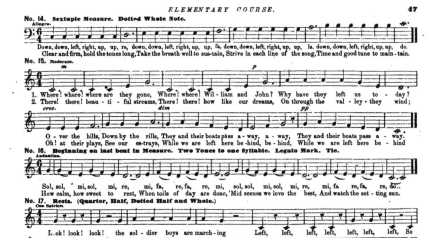

Down, down, left, right, up, up, re, down, down, left, right, up, up, fa, down, down, left, right, up, up, la. down, down, left, right, up, up, do.
Clear and firm, hold the tones long, Take the breath well to sus-tain, Strive in each line of the song, Time and good tune to main - tain.

No. 15. Moderato.

1. Where! where! where are they gone, Where! where! Wil - liam and John? Why have they left us to - day?
2. There! there! beau - ti - ful streams, There! there! how like our dreams, On through the val - ley - they wind;

O - ver the hills, Down by the rills, They and their boats pass a - way, a - way, They and their boats pass a - way.
Oh! at their plays, See our es-trays, While we are left here be -hind, be - hind, While we are left here be - hind

No. 16. Beginning on last beat in Measure. Two Tones to one Syllable. Legato Mark. Tie.

Sol, sol, mi, sol, mi, re, mi, fa, re, fa, re, mi, sol, sol, mi, sol, mi, re, mi, fa re, fa, re, do..
How calm, how sweet to rest, When toils of day are done, 'Mid scenes we love the best, And watch the set - ting sun.

No. 17. Rests. (Quarter, Half, Dotted Half and Whole.)
Con Spirito.

Look! look! look! the sol - dier boys are march - ing Left, left, left, left, left, left, left, So

on - ward all to - geth - er move, Un - til they hear the word they love, Halt! halt! halt!

No. 18.
Allegretto.
Free, clear tone. Prompt time.

1. O gai - ly the plow - man his ox - en is call - ing, Gee up! Gee up! Haw Bright, now come here.
2. A-round them the dead leaves are qui - et - ly fall - ing, How gay the day, How bright and how clear.

No. 19. Round. *First divide the class into two divisions, and let one come in after the other has sung one measure. Then divide into three, then into four, and so on to eight, each division coming in one after the other.*
Allegretto.

Now come on, you can - not catch us, For we have the start you know, Hear them say what we are say - ing, As we on to - geth - er go.

No. 20. Round. *This may have as many divisions as the preceding, but they must commence on the last half of the measure.*
Allegro.

Fol - low me, Fol - low me, Fol - low me, Fol - low me, Fol - low, fol - low, fol - low, fol - low, fol - low, fol - low, fol - low, fol - low me.

No. 21. Round. *This may also have as many divisions as it has meas- ures. Each beginning on the full measure.*
Allegretto.

Lit - tle Phil. Prise, when he o - pen'd his eyes, Said ha! ha! 'tis time to a - rise.

No. 22. Round. *As many divisions as measures*
Moderato.

Pip - ing up so clear and strong, Cuck - oo, Cuck - oo, hear the song.

No. 23. Round for three divisions.

John - ny! John - ny! What? what? So we keep call - ing him.

No. 24. Round for three divisions.

Pret - ty lit - tle May, Go not a - way, Oh, do stay.

No. 25. Round for four divisions.
Allegretto.

Now the black - smith's arm is swing - ing, And his cheer - ful song is sing - ing, Cling, cling, Clang, clang.

No. 26. Difference of Pitch between Male and Female Voice. Real Pitch of Clefs. Middle C. Brace.

Male voices sing in base clef, and female voices in treble, singing together only middle C.

Yes, you may take the low-er place, And we will soar a-loft in air, Ah!

Up-ward, up-ward thro' the base, yes!   Ah, hap-py you must be up   there.

No. 27.   *Male voices should not go above the added line—female voices should not go below the added line.*

Yes, we will sing it with-out fail, And you may fol-low, go-ing down,

Now af-ter us the up-ward scale,   Which we will do with-out a frown.

No. 28.   *Do not tresspass on each other's premises.*

We are sing-ing tre - ble,   sol, do, si, la, sol, fa, mi, re, do,   do, do.

Moderato.

We are sing-ing, on the base, we are sing-ing,   Do, sol, la, si, do, do.

No. 29.   Come with me where the sun-beams are spark-ling bright, Thro' mead-ows fair, Oh!

Come, come, Oh come,   4   Oh, come with me where all

No. 30. *Moderato.*   *Position. Breathing. Free tone. Articulation.*

Sol, fa, mi, re, do, si, la, sol, do, do, do, do, do, do, sol, fa, mi, re, do, si, la, sol, do, mi, sol, sol, do.

No. 31.   *When no dynamic marks are given, the words must indicate the proper strength.*

Though now al - to - geth - er, Still part - ed we must be; 'Tis bet - ter for the voi - ces, And for the har-mo - ny.

No. 32. *Moderato.*   m   p   *cres.................f*

When called a-while to part, How pleas-ant is the meet - ing, As near-er and near-er, At last we give the greet - ing.

No. 33.

Come up,   Come up,   Yes, yes, glad - ly, Do, si, la, &c

*Come down,   come down,   *Oh, yes,   yes,   glad - ly, Do, re, mi, &c.*

Extension of the Scale. Classification of the Voices. Tenor Clef.

No. 35. NOW ONCE MORE.

After singing this lesson, the class may sing "Anamosa" and "Rosalline," page 229.

No. 36. MUSIC.

Allegro. *When no dynamic marks are used, let the words indicate when the music should be loud, soft, increasing, diminishing, &c.*

1. Strike the harpstrings to thy praise, Spir - it of the Lyre! Soul of mel - o - dy, our lays By thy breath in - spire!

2. Sang the morn - ing stars when earth In the sun - light smiled, Sang the shep-herds, o'er the birth Of the Ho - ly Child;

3. Sing we then as Na - ture sings In her va - ried mood, As the hid - den for - est springs Glad the sol - i - tude;

From our Child-hood's ros - y spring, To Life's set-ting ray, Song is still the bless - ed thing, Cheer-ing all the way.

Ev - 'ry bless - ing, ev - 'ry tear, Song - ful ech - o craves, As for - ev - er in the ear, Is the song of waves.

As the rush - ing wa - ters sing, As the wild cas - cade, There is song in ev - 'ry-thing, That our God hath made.

After this, sing "Appledore," page 237, and "Almond" and "Ashmore," page 209.

No. 37.   OH, WHY SHOULD WE.

See that the quality of your tone is suited to express the words correctly. See "Theory of Music."

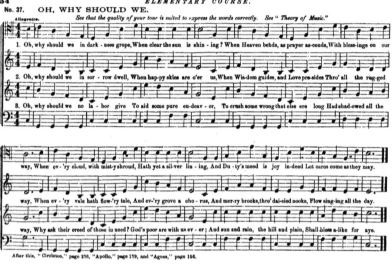

1. Oh, why should we in dark-ness grope, When clear the sun is shin-ing ? When Heaven behds, as prayer as-cends, With bless-ings on our

2. Oh, why should we in sor-row dwell, When hap-py skies are o'er us, When Wis-dom guides, and Love pre-sides Thro' all the rug-ged

3. Oh, why should we no la-bor give To aid some pure en-deav-or, To crush some wrong that else ere long Had shad-owed all the

way, When ev-'ry cloud, with mist-y shroud, Hath yet a sil-ver lin-ing, And Du-ty's meed is joy in-deed Let cares come as they may.

way, When ev-'ry vale hath flow-'ry tale, And ev-'ry grove a cho-rus, And mer-ry brooks, thro' dai-sied nooks, Flow sing-ing all the day.

way, Why ask their creed of those in need ? God's poor are with us ev-er ; And sun and rain, the hill and plain, Shall bless a-like for aye.

After this, " Circleton," page 276, "Apollo," page 119, and "Agnes," page 156.

No. 38. IN THE KEY OF G.

The Scale and Key of G, *See " Theory of Music and Teacher's Manual."*

1. G, G, F sharp, E, E, D, C, C, B, B, A, A, G, G, G, A, A, B, B, C, Give the pitch names full and free.

2. Now we're in the key of G, Fa, fa, mi, mi, re, re, do, Now sing up-ward first to C, High-er then our song shall go.

3. Eight, eight, seven, seven, six, six, five, Four, four, three, three, two, two, one; One, one, two, two, three, three, four, This is all, there are no more.

After practicing intervals in the key of G, sing " Eytinge," page 231.

No. 39. BASES AND TENORS.

Fa, sol, la, si, do, re, do, do, re, mi, fa, sol, la — sol, sol, sol, sol.

sol, sol, fa, mi

Do, re, mi, fa, sol, la, si, do, re, do, do, re, mi, fa, sol, la, sol, la, si, do.

Bass-es and Ten-ors sing up the first scale, Al-tos and Tre-bles con-tin-ue to sail, Up where the mu-sic is blow-ing a gale.

Do, re, mi, &c. After this sing "Cameo," page 182. sol, sol, sol, do.

No. 40. NOW, THE GLORIOUS DAY HAS COME.

This piece is especially adapted to a free delivery of the voice.   Words by "Paulina," written for this work.

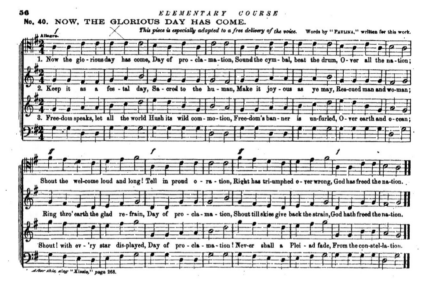

1. Now the glo - rious day has come, Day of pro - cla - ma - tion, Sound the cym - bal, beat the drum, O - ver all the na - tion;

2. Keep it as a fes - tal day, Sa - cred to the hu - man, Make it joy - ous as ye may, Res - cued man and wo - man;

3. Free-dom speaks, let all the world Hush its wild com - mo - tion, Free-dom's ban - ner is un-furled, O - ver earth and o - cean;

Shout the wel-come loud and long! Tell in proud o - ra - tion, Right has tri-umphed o - ver wrong, God has freed the na-tion.

Ring thro' earth the glad re - frain, Day of pro - cla - ma - tion, Shout till skies give back the strain, God hath freed the na-tion.

Shout! with ev - 'ry star dis-played, Day of pro - cla - ma - tion! Nev-er shall a Plei - ad fade, From the con-stel-la-tion.

After this, sing "Kinsie," page 268.

No. 41.   THE RIVER'S SONG.

1. Far a - way, far a - way in the sun - ny mead-ows, Hear it now, hear it now, 'tis the riv - er   song,

2. Long a - go, long a - go, sport-ed there sweet Child-hood, Hear it now, hear it now, shout-ing o'er the   wave,

3. On - ward still, on - ward still, is the riv - er glid-ing To the sea, to the sea, like the stream of   time,

Drip-ping, trip-ping, dash-ing, flash - ing, thro' the mer - ry shad-ows, Beau - ti - ful and mu - si - cal it glides a - long.

Quaf-fing, laugh-ing, sing-ing, spring-ing, Thro' the tan - gled wild-wood, O'er the rip - ples bend-ing, each young brow to   lave.

Surg - ing, urg - ing, swell-ing, tell - ing There is   no de - lay - ing, Mur-mur - ing of o - cean in a strain sub - lime.

After this, " Winona," page 270 (practice with treble and also on the same staff), and " Collyer," page 182 (practice two eighth notes

No. 42. BOAT SONG.

After this, "Clymer," page 211, "Clio," page 183,
and "Bellflower" and "Blue Island," page 157

No. 43. THE KEY OF D.

1. Do, do, si, si, la, la, sol, Key of D, This you see, Do, do, re, re, mi, mi, fa, All in time, Voi-ces chime.

2. 8, 8, 7, 7, 6, 6, 5, Tones should be Full and free, 1, 1, 2, 2, 3, 3, 4, Breath-ing too, Deep and true.

3. D, D, C sharp, B, and A, One and all, Now we call, D, D, E, E, F sharp, G, Join our band, Heart and hand.

After practicing in the upper scale and intervals in this key, sing "Freestone," page 232.

No. 44. GAILY OUR SONG.

1. Gai-ly our song, Float-eth a - long, Borne on the air of the beau-ti - ful day, Far in the dis-tance it di -eth a - way.

2. Let us be glad, Let none be sad, O-pen your heart to the sun-shine of song, Join in our mu-sic and help us a - long.

3. So ev-'ry day, All as we may, Hold our-selves read-y with hand and with heart, Each in his sta-tion to play well his part.

After this, sing "Father," page 215.

No. 45. THE SILVER FOUNTAIN.

1. Up-ward glanc-ing, laugh-ing, danc-ing, Is the sil-ver fount-ain; Hear the gen-tle mur-mur, As the spray-lets fall;

2. On the grass-es, tan-gled mass-es, All the noon-tide du-ring, Thus sweet cool-ing fin-gers Press the brow of care:

3. Thing of beau-ty, type of du-ty Is the sil-ver fount-ain, Spark-ling in the sun-beam, Cheer-ing in the gloom;

Ev-er cheer-y, nev-er wea-ry, In its beau-ty spring-ing, Glad-'ning and re-fresh-ing, bless-ing all.

Nev-er stay-ing, no de-lay-ing, Still some good pur-su-ing, Ben-i-son that fall-eth ev-'ry-where.

Thus for-ev-er, true en-deav-or, With its stead-y ra-diance, Shed-deth all a-round its light and bloom.

After this, " Blossom," page 254, and " De Vere," page 159.

No. 46. O, WHO IS DOWN IN THE WELL.

The altos commence with the exact pitch that the tenors leave.

1. O, who is down in the well so deep! Say who! say who! say who! O, yes, tell us, 'Tis

2. How came he down in the well so deep! Say how! say how! say how! O yes, tell us, He

3. How came he out of the well so deep! Say how! say how! say how! O yes, tell us, The

John - ny Lane, and he's fast a - sleep, That's who, yes, that's who, yes, that's who, ha! ha! ha!

tho't he'd rest on the wood - en sweep, That's how, yes, that's how, yes, that's how, ha! ha! ha!

place was cold, and he gave a leap, That's how, yes, that's how, yes, that's how, ha! ha! ha!

After preparing the minds for the change in sentiment, sing " Kennett," page 242, and " El Paso," page 185.

No. 47. IN THE KEY OF A.

Sol, la, si, do, re, mi, fa, sol,

Do, re, mi, fa, sol, la, si, do, In the key

Sol, la, si, do, In the key of

Do, re, mi, fa, sol, la, si, do.

Hark! hark! hark!   In the key of A we're sing-ing, Sweet the num-bers flow.

Hark! hark! hark!   In the key of A we're sing-ing, Sweet the num-bers flow.

A we're sing-ing, Hark! hark! hark! Do, sol, mi, In the key of A we're sing-ing, Sweet the num-bers flow.

After practicing intervals, sing "Ermine," page 239, and "Jerrold," page 215.

No. 48. LITTLE ONE, COME.

Repeat. Da Capo. Fine.

1. Lit - tle one, lit - tle one, o'er the lea, Trip a - long, skip a - long, come to me, Trill-ing a meas-ure with

D. C. O - ver the mead-ow, the vale, the lea, Flow-ers are spring-ing for you and me, Blos-soms are burst-ing on

2. Lit - tle one, lit - tle one, from the spray, War-ble the sing - ers, "A-way! a - way! Gath-er the blos-soms of

D. C. O - ver the riv - er, the lake and sea, Pin - ions are glanc-ing for you and me, Wave-lets are sing - ing a

FINE.

bird and bee, Trill-ing a song to me; { Mer-ri-ly, mer-ri-ly sing the lay, Mer-ri-ly, mer-ri-ly sing, / Au-tumn is gloom-y but Spring is gay, Hail to thee, hail to thee, Spring! }

ev - 'ry tree, Joy-ful it is to see.

morn and May, Gath-er and twine to-day." { Mer-ri-ly, mer-ri-ly trill the lay, Mer-ri-ly, mer-ri-ly sing, / Win-ter is fly-ing a - way, a - way, Hail to thee, hail to thee, Spring! }

round of glee, Joy-ful it is to see.

After this, "Hazel," page 187.

No. 49. OH! THE MERRY CHIME.

1. Oh! the mer-ry chime of the sum-mer time, In a blos-som la-den grove! Oh! the sweet love words to the
D. C. Oh! the mer-ry chime of the sum-mer time, Hath a mi-nor strain to me, For the sum-mers flow to the

2. Oh! the dear re-frain, to the heart a-gain, Is the old and plain-tive lay, When we marked the green, and the
D. C. Oh! the mer-ry chime of the sum-mer time, Hath a mi-nor strain to me, For the sum-mers flow to the

notes of birds, When the blue sky bends a-bove, { When the mow-ers come, from hill-side home, And chil-dren toss the hay; }
{ Till the blast of horn, on breeze is borne, And ech-o sings, "Aye, aye." }

long a-go, As the riv-ers to the sea.

blue be-tween, On the change-ful brow of May; { When the tir-ing glass, the lit-tle lass, Loved best was gur-gling brook, }
{ And when na-ture smiled on tru-ant child, As page of o-pen book; }

long a-go, As the riv-ers to the sea.

After this, " Ichamer," page 215.

No. 50. GLIDING ON.

Gliding on, gliding on, O'er the silent sea,

Gliding, gliding, glid - ing, glid - ing, O'er the calm and si - lent sea,

Gliding on, gliding on, O'er the calm and si - lent sea,

Glid - ing on, Glid - ing on, O'er the si - lent sea,

While our song, while our song Fills the air with mel - o - dy.

While our song,......... while our song......... Fills the air with mel - o - dy,

While our song, while our song, Fills the air with mel - o - dy.

While our song, while our song Fills the air with mel - o - dy.

After this, " Heath Hill," page 187, and " Castlemont," page 248.   5

No. 51. IN THE KEY OF E.

After this, "Murray's Chant," page 153, and "Ironville," page 189.

No. 52. FURTHER ON.

Words by J. R. Murray.

1. O the light shines down from the com-ing day, Fur-ther on! fur-ther on! And our hearts are glad as we
2. Let us all re-joice as we jour-ney still, Fur-ther on! Fur-ther on! See the warm bright beams break-ing
3. There's a bright-er day for our hearts to know, Fur-ther on! Fur-ther on! There's a sweet-er song than we

press our way, Fur-ther on! Fur-ther on! For Hope and Faith seemed well nigh past, And
o'er the hill, Fur-ther on! Fur-ther on! Let songs of joy our path-way cheer, While
sing be-low, Fur-ther on! Fur-ther on! Its beams shall chase a-way the night, Its

all our sky was o-ver-cast, But we see the bright morn-ing rise at last, Fur-ther on! fur-ther on!
Faith and Hope a-gain draw near, As we wait the day that will soon ap-pear, Fur-ther on! Fur-ther on!
mu-sic make our hearts grow light, As its gold-en rays burst up-on our sight, Fur-ther on! fur-ther on!

After this, anthem "Blessed is the people," page 302.

No. 53. FAIR AS THE MORNING.

Dotted Eighth and Sixteenth. Dotted Quarter.

1. Fair as the morn-ing, bright as the day, Vis-ion of beau-ty, fade not a-way; O-ver the mount-ain,

2. An-gel of slum-ber, bright as the day, Vis-ion of beau-ty, tar-ry for aye; Chase from the spir-it

3. Fain would I tell thee all I have known, Dream-ing and bless-ed wak-ing a-lone; Vis-ion of beau-ty

Chorus after each verse.

o - ver the sea, Come in sweet dreams to me. Far and wide the ech-oes roll a-long,

shad-ows of care, Leave but thy pres-ence there. Far and wide the ech-oes roll a-long,

tar-ry for me, Un-der the Dream-land tree. Far and wide the ech-oes roll a-long,

After this, "Andros," page 172, and "Appenine," page 180.

FAIR AS THE MORNING.—Concluded.

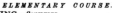

While the day world sings its bus-y song; But what are all its la-bors to me, Un-der the Dream-land tree?

No. 54. I KNOW A FAIRY BOWER.

From the "*Musical Curriculum.*"

1. { I know a fai-ry bow-er with-in the leaf-y dell, }
   { Where 'mid the wood-bine arch-es the mer-ry song-birds dwell; }

{ 'Tis sweet to hear their mu-sic, se-cure from sum-mer's heat, }
{ And pass the noon-tide hours..... with-in their cool re-treat }

D. C. { O come then to the bow-er with-in the leaf-y dell, }
      { Where 'mid the wood-bine arch-es, the mer-ry song-birds dwell. }

2. { The wild rose blush-es sweet-ly, and lifts her per-fum'd head }
   { When morn-ing wakes from slum-ber, and hours of life are fled. }

{ The sun-shine tries how vain-ly, to peep a-mid the leaves, }
{ With-in those love-ly arch-es, That na-ture bright-ly weaves. }

D. C. { O come then to the bow-er with-in the syl-van dell, }
      { Where na-ture's robes are bright-est, and mer-ry song-birds dwell. }

After this, "Barone," page 210

No. 60. IN THE KEY OF F.

1. In the key of F we sing, ha, ha, In the key of F we sing, ha, ha, We'll laugh and sing, ha,

2. Now the pitch names let us sing, ha, ha, Now the pitch names let us sing, ha, ha, F, E, D, C, ha

3. Now the scale names let us sing, ha, ha, Now the scale names let us sing, ha, ha, Eight, seven, six, five, ha,

ha, ha, ha, And mu - sic bring, ha, ha, ha, ha, We'll laugh and sing and mu - sic bring, ha, ha, ha, ha, ha, ha, ha.

ha, ha, ha, We all a - gree, ha, ha, ha, ha, We all a - gree, We all a - gree, ha, ha, ha, ha, ha, ha, ha, ha.

ha, ha, ha, For truth we'll strive, ha, ha, ha, ha, One, two, three, four, We'll sing no more, ha, ha, ha, ha, ha, ha, ha.

After this, "Banner," page 247, and chorus of "Oleander," page 160.

No. 56. THE BROOKLET.

Dal Segno.

From the "Musical Curriculum."

1. By the brook-let clear where the wil-low boughs sway, In the soft wind from the west, Are the grass-y slope and the

And the wil-low waves and the

2. Yes, the brook-let sings where the wil-low bends low, And my heart joins in the song, And the hap-py flow'rs on the

And it fans my cheek and it

FINE.

DAL SEGNO.

flow-ers so gay Of the home I love the best; O the soft wind from the pine hills comes with per-fume on its wings,

flow-ers look up, And the brook-let gai - ly sings.

grass-y slope glow, And I join their bright-eyed throng; Then the soft wind comes with per-fumed breath from off the west-ern hills,

kiss-es the flow'rs, And the wil - low branch-es fills.   After this, "Millmont," page 191, and anthem "Bless the Lord," page 306.

No. 57.   SING, BROTHERS, SING.   *From the "Musical Curriculum"*

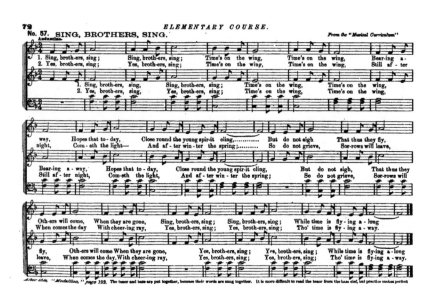

After this, "*Medallion*," *page 122.* The tenor and bass are put together, because their words are sung together. It is more difficult to read the tenor from the bass clef, but practice makes perfect

No. 58. **IN THE KEY OF B FLAT.**

After this, sing "Palace," page 167.

No. 59. SWIFTLY O'ER THE TIDE.   *From the "Musical Curriculum."*

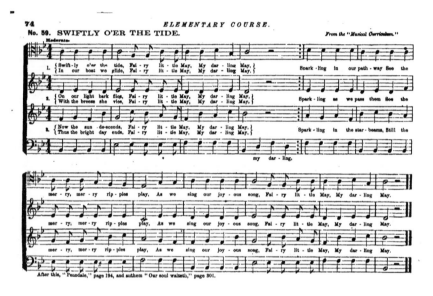

After this, "Penndale," page 194, and anthem "Our soul waiteth," page 301.

No. 80. WHERE IS WILLIE?

Tenderly.

Varieties of Measure.

Words and Music by JAMES R. MURRAY.

1. Where is my lit - tle one hid - ing to night? Wil - lie? Wil - lie?

2. Ah! but my heart is for - get - ting its pain, Wil - lie! Wil - lie! dar - ling,

3. Yet in the home that is o - ver the Sea, Wil - lie! dar - ling Wil - lie,

Come from your hid - ing place, lit - tle eyes bright! Wil - lie, Wil - lie, lov - ing and true.

Nev - er on earth shall I see thee a - gain, Wil - lie, Wil - lie, lov - ing and true.

Art thou not wait - ing with wel - come for me? Wil - lie, Wil - lie, lov - ing and true.

After explaining the different varieties of measure, sing " Pearl River," page 194, and " Newhope," page 220.

No. 61.   THE SILVER LAKE.   The key of E flat—(like the key of E in representation.)   From the "Musical Curriculum."

Moderato.

1. Come with me, the moon is beam-ing O'er the sil - ver wa - ters of the lake so fair; See ye not the

2. O de - lay not, time is fly - ing, And our com-rades call us from the peb - bly strand, E'en the gen - tle

3. Wake the harp to ac - cents ten - der, Soft - ly sweep the chords and war - ble sweet - est lays, While the star - ry

white sails gleam-ing, And the rip-ples laugh-ing in the sum - mer air? Come with me, the boat is wait-ing, And the

breeze is sigh-ing, As it waits to bear us from the dew - y land; 'Mid the hills in beau-ty gleam-ing, Still the

hosts in splen-dor, Greet their pla - cid mir - ror with an ear-nest gaze; Earth is heav'n in fair - est seem-ing, And the

After this, the chorus of "September," page 170, and "Trempeleau," page 197.

THE SILVER LAKE.—Concluded.

dis - tant voi - ces sweet-est ech-oes wake; Come, O come, the moon is beam-ing O'er the laugh-ing wa-ters of the sil-ver lake.

dis - tant voi - ces sweet-est ech-oes wake; Come, O come, the moon is beam-ing O'er the laugh-ing wa-ters of the sil-ver lake.

dis - tant voi - ces sweet-est ech-oes wake; Come, O come, the moon is beam-ing O'er the laugh-ing wa-ters of the sil-ver lake

No. 62. FAIRY LAND.

Words and Music by J. R. M.

1. Fai - ry land! fai - ry land! Come to me in dreams to-night; Fai-ry land! fai - ry land! Bring me treas-ures fair and bright.

2. Fai - ry land! fai - ry land! Come and soothe me in my sleep; Fai-ry land! fai - ry land! Bring me balm for eyes that weep.

3. Fai - ry land! fai - ry land! Give me loy-al friends tho' few; Fai-ry land! fai - ry land! Let my sweet-est dreams come true.

After this, " Delta," page 248, and " Renfrew," page 169.

No. 63. THE HILLSIDE. From the "Musical Curriculum."

The echo should be performed by four voices in another room, sufficiently closed or distant to make them sound like an echo. Let the last echo commence before the chorus closes.
After this, anthem "Thou will show me," page 304, "Vicar," page 196, and "Meredith," page 276.

No. 64.   Cadence Transposed into All the Keys.

This is the key of   C. Sol,   do, do. This is the key of   G. Sol,   do, do. This is the key of   D. Sol,   do, do. This is the key of

A. Sol,   do, do. This is the key of   E. Sol,   do, do. This is the key of   B. Sol,   do, do. This is the key of

F sharp, and   al - so   G flat, the key of   G flat. Sol, sol,   do. This is the key of   D flat. Sol, sol,   do.

This is   the key of   A flat. Sol, sol,   do. This is the key of   E flat. Sol, sol,   do. This is the key of

B flat. Sol, sol,   do. This is the key of   F. Sol,   do, do. Home a - gain to the key of C, to the key, to the key of C.

No. 65. The Major Scales.

The following lesson should be sung with syllables and also with different vowel sounds sometimes crescendo and diminuendo, and sometimes staccato and sometimes giving different qualities of tone. When the scale is too high, take the octave below. Sing from beginning to end without stopping, passing from one key to the next in perfect time.

Do, re, mi, fa, sol, la, si, do, si, la, sol, fa, mi, re, do, mi, sol, do, sol, mi, do.   Do, re, mi, fa, sol, la, si, do, si, la, sol, fa, mi, re, do, mi, sol, do, sol, mi, do.

Do, re, mi, fa, sol, la, si, do, si, la, sol, fa, mi, re, do, mi, sol, do, sol, mi, do.   Do, re, mi, fa, sol, la, si, do, si, la, sol, fa, mi, re, do, mi, sol, do, sol, mi, do.

Do, re, mi, fa, sol, la, si, do, si, la, sol, fa, mi, re, do, mi, sol, do, sol, mi, do.   Do, re, mi, fa, sol, la, si, do, si, la, sol, fa, mi, re, do, mi, sol, do, sol, mi, do.

Do, re, mi, fa, sol, la, si, do, si, la, sol, fa, mi, re, do, mi, sol, do, sol, mi, do.   Do, re, mi, fa, sol, la, si, do, si, la, sol, fa, mi, re, do, mi, sol, do, sol, mi, do.

Do, re, mi, fa, sol, la, si, do, si, la, sol, fa, mi, re, do, mi, sol, do, sol, mi, do.   Do, re, mi, fa, sol, la, si, do, si, la, sol, fa, mi, re, do, mi, sol, do, sol, mi, do.

Do, re, mi, fa, sol, la, si, do, si, la, sol, fa, mi, re, do, mi, sol, do, sol, mi, do.   Do, re, mi, fa, sol, la, si, do, si, la, sol, fa, mi, re, do, mi, sol, do, sol, mi, do.

Each scale is a *fifth* from the preceding one, excepting the scale of G flat, which is at the same pitch with the one that precedes it (F sharp). This difference in *signs*, but not in *sound*, is called an enharmonic difference.

Transposing by fourths should also be practiced. This takes you through the flats first, and back through the sharps.

INTERMEDIATE COURSE.

No. 66. 'COME JOIN OUR HAPPY THRONG.'

H. R. PALMER.
From the "Song Queen," by permission.

Allegretto. Sharp Four. (See " Theory of Music, page 80.) FINE.

1. Come join our hap-py, hap-py throng, Dear friends sing this mer-ry, mer-ry song, While thus we the har-mo-ny pro-long, Come friends join our lay.
D.C. When all thus mer-ri-ly u-nite, Our sing-ing will ev-er give de-light, And all e - vil tho'ts will put to flight, Then sing while we may.

2. Join na-ture's mer-ry round-de-lay, Thro' wood-land and mead-ows let us stray, And pass pleas-ant-ly the hours a-way, Then join, join us all.
D.C. Thus na-ture plays her fai-ry lyre, Decked out in her hol-i-day at-tire, In - vites us her love-li-ness to share, Then haste to her call.

D. C.

Yes, we will join the mer-ry strain, While thus we meet hap-pi-ly a-gain, And dull care we'll cheer-ful-ly re-sign, On this fes-tive day.

Sweet flow'rs will greet us as we go, All smil-ing with ti-ny drops of dew, Their fra-grance and beau-ty ev-er now, Our hearts will en - thrall.

After this, "Advance" and "Annabel," page 155; and "St. Catherine," page 255.

(81)

6

No. 67. O, THE QUEEN OF NIGHT IS RISING.

Flat Seven. Changing Key.

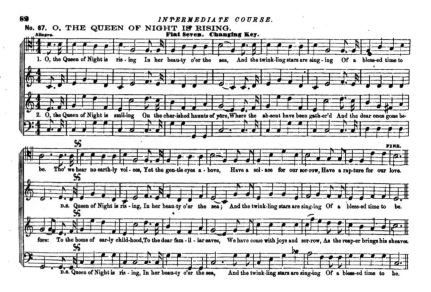

O, THE QUEEN OF NIGHT IS RISING.—Concluded.

The moon-beams are glanc-ing O'er for-est, lake and lea, The wave-lets are danc-ing With mu-sic wild and free; Yes, yes, the

The moon-beams are glanc-ing O'er for-est, lake and lea, The wave-lets are danc-ing With mu-sic wild and free; Yes, yes, the

DAL SEGNO

moon-beams are glanc-ing, And list! the sound-ing sea, Our hearts all en - tranc - ing With mys-tic mel - o - dy. O, the

moon-beams are glanc-ing, And list! the sound-ing sea, Our hearts all en - tranc - ing With mys-tic mel - o - dy. O, the

After this, anthem, "Lift up your heads," page 306.

No. 68.   BUILDING OF THE MINOR SCALE.

1. *Tones one, two and three.*

La, la, si, si, do, do, si, si, la, la, si, si, do, do, si, si, la.

2.

La, si, do, si, la, si, do, si, la, si, do, si, la, si, do, si, la.

3. *Tones one, two, three, four and five.*

La, la, si, si, do, do, re, re, mi, mi, mi, re, re, do, do, si, si, la.

4.

La, si, do, re, mi, re, do, si, la, si, do, re, mi, re, do, si, la.

5. *Tones one, two, three, four, five and six.*

La, si, do, do, re, re, mi, mi, fa, mi, mi, fa, fa, mi, re, do, si, la.

6.

La, si, do, re, mi, fa, mi, fa, mi, fa, mi, fa, mi, re, do, si, la.

7. *Tones eight and seven.*

La, la, si, si, la, la, si, si, la, mi, mi, fa, fa, mi, mi, fa, fa, mi.

8.

La, si, la, mi, fa, mi, la, si, la, si, la, mi, fa, mi, fa, mi.

9. *The principal difficulty is from six to seven or vice versa.*

La, si, la, si, la, fa, mi, fa, mi, fa, mi, mi, la, si, la.

10.

La, si, la, si, fa, mi, fa, mi, la, si, fa, mi, la, si, fa, mi.

11.

Mi, mi, fa, mi, fa, si, si, la, si, la, fa, mi, si, si, la.

12.

Mi, mi, fa, fa, si, si, la, mi, mi, fa, fa, si, si, la.

13.

La, la, si, si, do, do, re, re, mi, mi, fa, fa, si, si, la.

14.

La, la, si, si, fa, fa, mi, mi, re, re, do, do, si, si, la.

15.

La, si, do, re, mi, fa, si, la, la, si, fa, mi, re, do, si, la.

16.

La, si, do, re, mi, fa, si, la, la, si, fa, mi, re, do, si, la.

After this—*Arcadone, page 343; Ballerale, page 180; Curwen, page 200; Ballentine, page 210; and Artwall, page 247.*

No. 69. "GENTLY SIGHS THE BREEZE."

H. R. Palmer.

From the "Song Queen," by permission.

Moderato. SOLO, or SEMI-CHORUS. *For the practice of the Triplet.*

1. Gen-tly, gen - tly sighs the breeze, As it floats a-mong the trees; Like a voice of ser-aph bright, Sing-ing to the world good-night.
2. Gen-tly, gen - tly sighs the breeze, As it floats a-mong the trees; Like a voice of ser-aph bright, Sing-ing to the world good-night.

CHORUS, Subdued. *(Sing throughout "la" through the entire Chorus rather staccato.)*

La, la, la, la, la, &c.

La, la, la, la, la, &c.

La, la, la, la, la, &c.

Ev-'ry hill and ev - 'ry glade, In the twi-light seems to fade; While the whis-p'ring breez-es say Or - i - sons for close of day.
Now the birds are gone to rest, O'er the earth night, sa - ble drest, Hides her beau ties from our sight; We, dear friends, must bid good-night.

After this, Hymn, "We shall Know," page 296; Dixfield and Derringford, page 184; and Dear Home, page 212.

No. 70. JUST LIKE LOVE.

Sharp Four and Flat Seven.

P. P. Bliss.

JUST LIKE LOVE.—Concluded.

After this—"Cheyenne," page 183; "Content and Cluster," page 188; and Anthem, "The Lord is Good," page 305.

No. 71.   LIGHT AND SHADE.   E Minor.

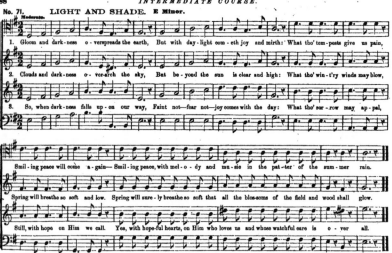

1. Gloom and dark-ness o-verspreads the earth, But with day-light com-eth joy and mirth: What tho' tem-pests give us pain,

2. Clouds and dark-ness o-ver-arch the sky, But be-yond the sun is clear and high: What tho' win-t'ry winds may blow,

3. So, when dark-ness falls up-on our way, Faint not—fear not—joy comes with the day: What tho' sor-row may ap-pal,

Smil-ing peace will come a-gain— Smil-ing peace, with mel-o-dy and mu-sic in the pat-ter of the sum-mer rain.

Spring will breathe so soft and low. Spring will sure-ly breathe so soft that all the blos-soms of the field and wood shall glow.

Still, with hope on Him we call. Yes, with hope-ful hearts, on Him who loves us and whose watchful care is o-ver all.

After this—"Darrow," page 184 ; "Castellan," page 158 ; "Clare," page 211 ; and Anthem "Give ear, O Shepherd," page 313.

No. 72. WHISTLING FARMER BOY.

Geo. F. Root.
From "Forest Choir."

Allegretto.

1. See the mer - ry farm - er - boy Tramp the mead-ows thro'; Swing his hoe in care - less joy, While dash-ing off the dew:

2. When the farm-er - boy, at noon, Rests be-neath the shade, List-'ning to the cease-less tune, That's thrill-ing thro' the glade;

3. When the bus - y day's em-ploy Ends at dew - y eve, Then the hap - py farm - er - boy Doth haste his work to leave;

Bob - o - link in ma - ples high Trills his notes of glee; Farm - er - boy a gay re - ply, Now whis - tles cheer - i - ly.

Long and loud the har-vest fly Winds his bu - gle 'round; Long, and loud, and shrill and high, He whis - tles back the sound.

Trudg-ing down the qui - et vale, Climb-ing o'er the hill, Whis-tling back the change-less wail Of plain - tive Whip-poor-will.

Interlude, to be whistled.

Piano or Organ.

4. Farmer-boy is blithe and gay,
   Morning, noon or night;
   Song or glee or roundelay,
   He's whistling with delight:
   Merry heart, so full of glee,
   Over-full of fun !
   Hear him whistling merrily

SEE-SAW.

F. W. Root.

1. Life is a see - saw board—how we go A - way to the skies all sun-ny; Downward, and never so

2. He who ex - ults on the up - ward plank Too high for a re - cog - ni - tion, (Having near sight) has the

3. One and an - oth - er are fall - ing still From ends that are near - est Heav - en; Friends who were faithful thro'

swift, so low, As when we have lost our mon-ey. Life is a see-saw board—friend and foe, Here - a - way, there - a - way,

poor to thank For gain - ing his proud po - si - tion. Life is a see-saw board—friend and foe, Here - a - way, there - a - way,

good and ill, And foes we have late for - giv - en. Life is a see-saw board—friend and foe, Here - a - way, there - a - way,

— 185. and " Fontleroy " and " Flotow," page 186.

SEE-SAW.—Concluded.

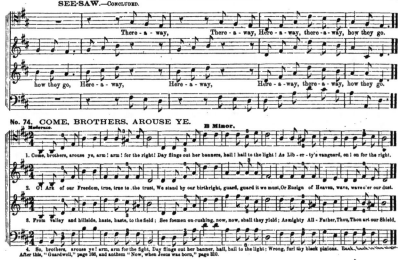

There - a - way, There - a - way, Here - a - way, there - a - way, how they go.

how they go, Here - a - way, Here - a - way, Here - a - way, there - a - way, how they go.

No. 74. COME, BROTHERS, AROUSE YE.

B Minor.

1. Come, brothers, arouse ye, arm! arm! for the right! Day flings out her banners, hail! hail to the light! As Lib - er - ty's vanguard, on! on for the right.

2. O! Ark of our Freedom, true, true to the trust, We stand by our birthright, guard, guard it we must, Or Ensign of Heaven, wave, wave o'er our dust.

3. From valley and hillside, haste, haste, to the field; See foemen on-rushing, now, now, shall they yield; As mighty All - Father, Thou, Thou art our Shield.

4. So, brothers, arouse ye! arm, arm for the fight, Day flings out her banner, hail, hail to the light; Wrong, furl thy black pinions. Back, back to the night.

After this, "Guardwell," page 186, and anthem "Now, when Jesus was born," page 310.

No. 75.   **AWAY, AWAY, THE TRACK IS WHITE.**

Published in Sheet Form with Accompaniment.

Words by EMILY HUNTINGTON MILLER.

1. A - way! a - way! the track is white, The stars are shi - ning clear to night, The win - ter winds are sleep - ing; The moon a - bove the stee - ple tall, A sil - ver cres-cent o - ver all, Her si - lent watch is keep - ing Her si - lent watch is

2. A - way! a - way! our hearts are gay, And need not breathe by night or day A sigh for sum - mer pleas - ure; The mer - ry bells ring gai - ly out, Our lips keep time with song and shout, And laugh in hap-py meas - ure, And laugh in hap - py

3. A - way! a - way! a - cross the plain, We sweep as sea - birds skim the main, Our puls-es gai - ly leap - ing; The stars are bright the track is white, There's joy in ev - 'ry heart tonight, While win-ter winds are sleep - ing, While win-ter winds are

After this, "Hibbard" and "Ines," Hymn page 188, and "Julian," page 216.

AWAY, AWAY, THE TRACK IS WHITE. Concluded.

Some Sleigh Bells, keeping time with the music and a few Torpedos, to imitate the crack of the whip, will make the Chorus still more effective.

No. 76.   THERE'S A WITCHING LIGHT IN THE STARS TO-NIGHT.

Words by MATTIE WINFIELD TORREY.   *Sing first four lines every time in Da Capo for a chorus.*   Music by J. R. MURRAY.

After this, "Junaliska" and "Keyesville," page 216, "Freeland," "Hawthorndell," and "Grand Vision," page 161.

No. 77.   THERE'S NO TIME LIKE THE PRESENT TIME.

Sing the large words every time in the D. C. for a chorus.

Words by E. E. REXFORD.   Music by JAMES R. MURRAY.

1. There's no time like the present time; The future is not ours; If we would make our lives sublime, Improve the present hours.

2. There's no time like the pres-ent time; The deeds we do to - day, May make our mem - o - ries sub-lime, When we have pass'd a - way.

3. There's no time like the pres-ent time, For do-ing kind - ly deeds, And gath'ring in a gen-'rous store To serve our future needs;

For oh! how lit - tle can we tell What fu-ture hours may bring; So, if we use the pres-ent well, Our past shall bear no sting, For oh!

The pre-sent is the time to build The structure of our past; Let ev-'ry stone and tile be made Of deeds and thoughts to last, For oh!

To-day we write a page of life The fu-ture shall un-fold; But let there be no tale of strife, No dross a-mong the gold, For oh!

No. 78.   SONG IN SUNSHINE.

Melody by Miss M. R. Morton.

1. Sing a - way, ye joy-ous birds, While the sun is o'er us! If I on - ly know your words I would swell the cho - rus:

2. Soft - ly as an an-gel's wing Comes an in - spi - ra - tion: Oh, that my poor soul could sing Wor - thy of cre - a - tion!

3. I would sound a note of joy, Thro' the vales o' Dev - on, Sweet as love's when he a boy New - ly came from heav - en;

Sing ye warblers of the sky! Sing, ye hap - py thrush - es! And ye lit - tle ones that lie Down a - mong the rush - es.

Like the sol-emn chant-ing tree, Na - ture in de - vo - tion: Like the mer - ry, harp-ing bee, Har - mo - ny in mo - tion

Till the bu - sy world be-guiled With its ech - oes ring - ing, Shouted, "Hark! for Na-ture's child Her own song is sing - ing"

After this—"Myron," "Minneiska," "Maroan Lea," page 164 ; and "Israella," page 180.

SONG IN SUNSHINE.—Concluded.

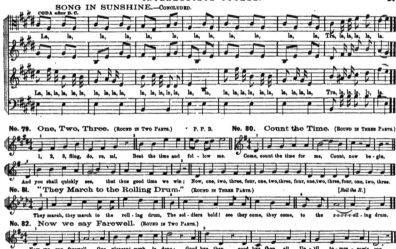

La, la, la, la, la, la, la, la, la, la, la, la, Tra, la, la, la, la, la.

La, la, la, la, la, la, la, la, la, la, la, la, la, la, la, la, la, la, la, la, la, la, la, la, Tra, la, la, la, la, la.

No. 79. One, Two, Three. (Round in Two Parts.)   P. P. B.   No. 80. Count the Time. (Round in Three Parts.)

1, 2, 3, Sing, do, re, mi, Beat the time and fol - low me.   Come, count the time for me, Count, now be - gin,

And you shall quickly see, that thus good time we win; Now, one, two, three, four, one, two, three, four, one, two, three, four, one, two, three.

No. 81. "They March to the Rolling Drum." (Round in Three Parts.)   [Roll the R.]

They march, they march to the roll - ing drum, The sol - diers bold! see they come, they come, to the r-r-r-r-r-oll - ing drum.

No. 82. Now we say Farewell. (Round in Two Parts.)

Now we say farewell, Our pleasant work is done: Good bye, then, good bye then all Un - till to - mor - row's sun.

7

No. 83. WHEN MY SHIP COMES IN.

Moderato.

Geo. Haywood. Arranged by G. F. R.

Publish-d in sheet form with accompaniment.

1. When my ship comes in, I will have me a home By the shore of the dark blue sea, }
In the qui - et depths of the shad - ow - y woods Of the land of the brave and free; } I will build me a cot on the
D. C. When the winds are wild on the bil - low - y sea, In the beau - ty of night and storm.

2. For the wan-d'rer sad a re - treat shall there be, And a loaf for the hun-gry poor; }
And mis - for - tune's child-ren a wel-come shall meet, When they come to our o - pen door; } And we'll nev - er for-get all the
D. C. The pro - tect - ing hand of the Friend ev - er near, Of the Fa - ther and Friend of all.

D. C.   *CHORUS, after D. C.*

moss - y cliff, Where the breeze comes balm-y and warm; When my ship comes in, when my ship comes in, With the gal - lant treas-ure that she

lov - ing care, Wheth-er weal or woe shall be-fall, When my ship comes in, when my ship comes in, With the gal - lant treas-ure that she

bears for me, What a home I'll have, when my ship comes in From the far off isles of the sound-ing sea.

bears for me, What a home I'll have, when my ship comes in From the far off isles of the sound-ing sea.

3. As the months and years shall be rolling away,
Our endeavor and aim shall be,
All the wrong to shun, and the right to pur-
sue,
And we'll learn from the wond'rous sea,
That if clouds, and the storm and the wreck
shall come
We shall know that sorrow and pain,
Like the ocean storm, may endure for a night,
But the sunshine will come again.

Chorus—When my ship comes in, &c.

After this, "Because He Loved Me So," page 286; "Jesus by the Sea," page 284; "Manitou," page 191.

No. 84. SWEETLY THRO' THE SILENCE. Words by MATTIE WINFIELD TORREY. Music by J. R. MURRAY.

Moderato.

1. Its spell is on me now, My heart beats quick and fast; Joy's light a-round my brow, By mu-sic's voice, is cast :}
For, O, they thrill the heart That naught can charm be-side; Those mag-ic tones which start The air of e-ven-tide. }

2. 'Tis sad, and then 'tis gay, 'Tis loud and soft-ly sweet; A sound that sinks a-way in mur-murs at my feet :}
And now a wild-er strain, A more im-pas-sion'd flow, A wail, as if of pain, A sob, as if of woe. }

CHORUS. (Observe the crescendo and diminuendo, as indicated by the words of the Chorus.)

Sweet-ly thro' the si-lence, thro' the si-lence steal-ing, How the ech - o swells, it dies, it swells, it dies,

Sweet—ly thro' the si-lence, thro' the si-lence steal-ing, How the ech - o swells, dies, swells, dies,

Sweet - ly through the si - lence steal-ing, Hear the ech-o swell, it dies, it swells, it dies, it swells, it dies,

Sweet-ly thro' the si-lence, thro' the si-lence steal-ing, How the ech - o swells, dies, swells, dies,

Sound-ing like the dis-tant, like the dis-tant peal-ing Of sweet mem-'ry bells, sweet mem-'ry bells.

Sound ing like the dis-tant, like the dis-tant peal-ing Of sweet mem-'ry bells, sweet mem-'ry bells.

Sound - ing like the dis - tant peal-ing Of sweet mem-'ry bells.

Sound ing like the dis-tant, like the dis-tant peal-ing Of sweet mem-'ry bells, sweet mem-'ry bells.

3. And now it dies away,
Of its own sweetness dies,
As the last beam of day
Is fading from the skies;
Yet, on the air of night
There lingers yet the sigh
That tells our darken'd sight
Where music pass'd us by.

Chorus—Sweetly through, &c.

After this, "Oakwood," page 166; "Natalie," page 192; "Our Beautiful Home," page 295.

No. 85.   Allegretto.   CAN YOU SING?

Words and Music by P. P. Bliss.

1. Can you sing? Then sing, Sing a - way, Sing well: You may sing a song to night, That will
2. Can you laugh? Then laugh, Laugh a - way, Laugh well: You may laugh if you are poor: Wis - er
3. Can you work? Then work, Work a - way, Work well: Here be - gin your works of love, If the

tell for Truth and Right, You may sing some bur - den light, Who can tell? Then sing, Sing a-
ones have laughed be - fore, You may live to laugh the more, Who can tell? Then laugh, Laugh a-
Mas - ter doth ap - prove, You may fin - ish them a - bove, Who can tell? Then work, Work a-

CHORUS.

1. Then sing,
2. Then laugh,
3. Then work.

way, Sing a - way, Sing a - way, Sing well; You may sing some bur - den light, Who can tell?
way, Laugh a - way, Laugh a - way, Laugh well; You may live to laugh the more, Who can tell?
way, Work a - way, Work a - way, Work well; You may fin - ish them a - bove, Who can tell?

No. 86.
COME OVER THE LAKE.

Words and Music by J. R. MURRAY

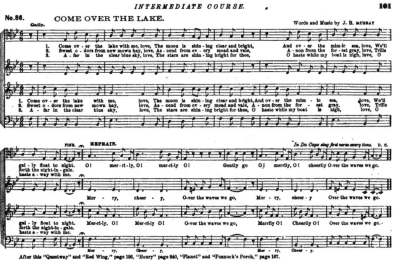

After this "Questway" and "Red Wing," page 195, "Henry," page 240, "Planet" and "Pennock's Porch," page 167.

No. 87.   THE FARMER'S SONG. (Quartet and Chorus.)   Words and Chorus by B. R. Hanby.

1. Up the steeps the morn is bound-ing, Hark! the milk-maid's song is sound-ing, Voice of bird and bee re-sound-ing; Up my lads, be blithe as they.

2. Now, while earth and sky are glow-ing, Speed the plow-ing, speed the mow-ing, Gay the song that cheers our go-ing; Glad-ly toil we while we may.

3. Now the west-ern sun de-scend-ing, Shad-ows with the light are blend-ing; Lo! the herds are homeward wend-ing; Cease the toil, but not the lay.

CHORUS. *Allegretto.*

Cheer-i-ly, cheer-i-ly, we heed the call, heed the call, heed the call; Cheer-i-ly, cheer-i-ly we

Mer-ri-ly, mer-ri-ly, we hast-en all, hast-en all, hast-en all; Mer-ri-ly, mer-ri-ly we

THE FARMER'S SONG.—Concluded.

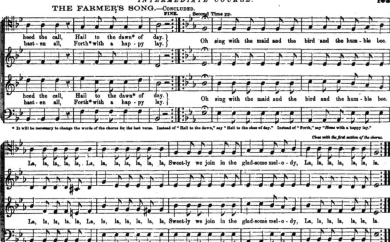

heed the call, Hail to the dawn* of day. }
hast-en all, Forth* with a hap-py lay. }
Oh sing with the maid and the bird and the hum-ble bee.

heed the call, Hail to the dawn* of day. }
hast-en all, Forth* with a hap-py lay. }
Oh sing with the maid and the bird and the hum-ble bee.

* It will be necessary to change the words of the chorus for the last verse. Instead of " Hail to the dawn," say " Hail to the close of day." Instead of " Forth," say *"Home with a happy lay."*

Close with the first section of the chorus.

La, la, la, la, la, La, la, la, la, la, la, Sweet-ly we join in the glad-some mel-o-dy, La, la, la, la, la, la, la.

La, la, la, la, la, La, la, la, la, la, la, Sweet-ly we join in the glad-some mel-o-dy, La, la, la, la, la, la, la.

After this—"Dyerton," "Carino " and " Doyanne," page 338 ; " Ophinett," " Orland's Rest " and " Nectarine," page 221 ; and " Nilsen," page 220.

No. 88. SAIL ON, MY BARK. C. M. WYMAN.

1. Sail on, sail on, thou fearless bark, Wher-ev-er blows the welcome wind; It can-not lead to scenes more dark—more sad than those we

2. Sail on, sail on thro' endless space, Thro' calm, thro' tempest stop no more; The stormiest sea's a rest-ing place, To him who leaves such

leave be-hind. Each wave that pass-es seems to say, Tho' death beneath our smile may be Less cold we are, less false than they Whose

hearts on shore. Or if some des-ert land we meet, Where nev-er yet false heart-ed men Pro-faned a world that else were sweet. Then

No. 89. LITTLE ACTS OF KINDNESS. T. Martin Towne.

Allegretto.

smil-ing wreck'd thy hopes and thee.

rest thee, bark, but not till then.

1. Lit-tle acts of kindness, Tri-fling though they are, How they seem to bright-en

2. Lit-tle acts of kindness, How they cheer the heart! What a world of glad-ness

3. Lit-tle acts of kindness, Noth-ing do they cost: Yet when they are want-ing

This dark world of care! Lit-tle acts of kindness, O, how po-tent they, To dis-pel the shad-ows Of life's cloud-y day.

Will a smile im-part! How a gen-tle ac-cent Calms the troubled soul, When the waves of pas-sion O'er it wild-ly roll.

Life's best charm is lost! Lit-tle acts of kindness, Rich-est gems of earth, Though they seem but tri-fles, Price-less is their worth.

After this—"Oliver," "Plimpton" and "Quinlan," page 228; and Hymn, "Savior and Friend," page 290.

No. 90. FOREST ECHOES.

3. They floated down thro' the list'ning silence,
   Like tones of a silver dream;   [sorrow,
   From realms far away where there was no
   By life's unruffled stream:
      Hark! echo sweet, &c.

4. And evermore, thro' the silent marches,
   Where life's busy moments throng,
   I hear far away in the quiet shadows,
     Those blissful notes of song.
      Hark! echoes sweet, &c.

* If convenient, let four clear, true voices in another room, sing the echo—shutting themselves up, until the imitation is correct. The last echo should commence a little before the chorus finish their last word.

No. 91.   SEE THE SNOW COME DOWN.   *Words and Music by J. R.* MURRAY.

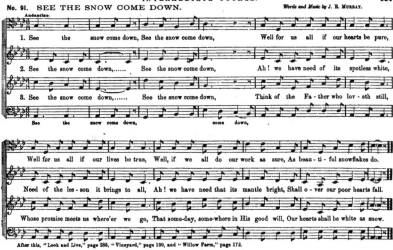

1. See   the   snow come down, See the snow come down,   Well for us all if our hearts be pure,
2. See   the snow come down,...... See the snow come down,   Ah ! we have need of its spotless white,
3. See   the snow come down,...... See the snow come down,   Think of the Fa-ther who lov-eth still,

See   the   snow come down,   come   down,

Well for us all if our lives be true, Well, if we all do our work as sure, As beau-ti-ful snowflakes do.
Need of the les-son it brings to all, Ah ! we have need that its mantle bright, Shall o-ver our poor hearts fall.
Whose promise meets us where'er we go, That some-day, some-where in His good will, Our hearts shall be white as snow.

After this, "Look and Live," page 285, "Vineyard," page 199, and "Willow Farm," page 172.

108 No. 92. WORDS OF KINDNESS. J. R. MURRAY.

WORDS OF KINDNESS.—Concluded.

After this, "Wabash Avenue," page 172, "Rhineland," page 223, "Wilding," page 172, "Yare Valley," page 201. Also, in the key of D flat, "Yelam" and 'Zinda," page 201, and "Tourjee," page 223.

No. 93.   GOOD NIGHT.

No. 94. The Minor Scales.

Observe the directions for singing these scales that are given for the Major Scales on page 80.

La, si, do, re, mi, fa, si, la, si, fa, mi, re, do, si, la, do, mi, la, mi, do, la.

La, si, do, re, mi, fa, si, la, si, fa, mi, re, do, si, la, do, mi, la, mi, do, la.

La, si, do, re, mi, fa, si, la, si, fa, mi, re, do, si, la, do, mi, la, mi, do, la.

La, si, do, re, mi, fa, si, la, si, fa, mi, re, do, si, la, do, mi, la, mi, do, la.

La, si, do, re, mi, fa, si, la, si, fa, mi, re, do, si, la, do, mi, la, mi, do, la.

La, si, do, re, mi, fa, si, la, si, fa, mi, re, do, si, la, do, mi, la, mi, do, la.

La, si, do, re, mi, fa, si, la, si, fa, mi, re, do, si, la, do, mi, la, mi, do, la.

La, si, do, re, mi, fa, si, la, si, fa, mi, re, do, si, la, do, mi, la, mi, do, la.

La, si, do, re, mi, fa, si, la, si, fa, mi, re, do, si, la, do, mi, la, mi, do, la.

La, si, do, re, mi, fa, si, la, si, fa, mi, re, do, si, la, do, mi, la, mi, do, la.

La, si, do, re, mi, fa, si, la, si, fa, mi, re, do, si, la, do, mi, la, mi, do, la.

La, si, do, re, mi, fa, si, la, si, fa, mi, re, do, si, la, do, mi, la, mi, do, la.

ADVANCED COURSE.

HOME AGAIN RETURNING.

(Published in sheet form.)

Words by Mattie Winfield Torrey.   G. F. R

1. We have wan - dered long from the house-hold throng, From the old fa - mil - iar pla - ces,
2. Tho' the winds are light and the skies are bright In the land where we've been stray - ing,
3. How our heart still clings to the sim - ple things We have loved in days long van - ished!

And our hearts are light with our
Tho' the clime is fair and a
Ere our lives grew cold, and our

joy to - night, As we greet your smil - ing fa - ces,   From our na - tive shore we will roam no more While the
balm - y air With its sum - mer flow'rs is play - ing,   Yet our hearts turned still, with a right good will, To the
hearts felt old, Or the dreams of youth were ban - ished!   We have wan - dered far, but our guid - ing star, O'er the

bright skies bend a - bove us;   Naught shall tempt our feet from our blest re - treat, With the friends who tru - ly
land be - yond the o - cean;   And we breathed its name and we sang its fame With a tide of sweet e -
West - ern wa - ters burn - ing,   Sheds its star - ry light on our dark - est night, And we're home a - gain re -

HOME AGAIN RETURNING.—Concluded.

love us. Home re - turn - ing nev - er more from thee to stray,.
mo - tion.
turn - ing !

Oh, we are home a - gain re - turn - ing, home a - gain re - turn - ing, Nev-er more to wan-der from our hap-py land a - way,

Oh, we are home a - gain re - turn - ing, home a - gain re - turn - ing, Nev-er more to wan-der from our hap-py land a - way,

Home a - gain home a - gain, Oh, joy - ful lay.

Oh, we're home a - gain re - turn - ing home a - gain re - turn - ing, Pour it forth with thankful hearts, the joy - ful, joy-ful lay.

Oh, we're home a - gain re - turn - ing home a - gain re - turn - ing, Pour it forth with thankful hearts, the joy - ful, joy-ful lay.

HAIL OUR NATAL MORN!

Maestoso.

H. R. PALMER.

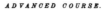

1. Hail our coun-try's na-tal morn! Hail our spread-ing kin-dred born! Hail thou ban-ner not yet torn! Still wav-ing o'er the FREE!
2. Who would sev-er Free-dom's shrine? Who would draw th'in-vid-ious line? Though by birth one spot be mine, Yet dear is all the rest;
3. By our al-tars pure and free, By our law's deep-root-ed tree, By the past dread mem-o-ry, And by our MAR-TYRS slain;

While, this day, in fes-tal throng, Mil-lions swell the pat-riot song, Shall not we thy notes pro-long? Hal-low'd ju-bi-lee!
Dear to me the SOUTH's fair land, Dear the cen-tral mount-ain band, Dear NEW ENG-LAND's rock-y strand, Dear the prai-ried WEST.
By our com-mon pa-rent tongue, By our hopes, bright, buoy-ant, young, By the tie of coun-try strong, U-nit-ed we'll re-main.

CHORUS.

Hail! all hail! Hail! all hail! Hail! all hail! Still wav-ing o'er the free.

Hail our coun-try's na-tal morn, Hail ye mil-lions yet un-born; Hail thou ban-ner yet un-torn, Still wav-ing o'er the free.

Hail! all hail! Hail! all hail! Hail! all hail! Still wav-ing o'er the free.

8

A SWEET LITTLE CHILD.

Words by REV. G. HARTLEY.   Music by T. MARTIN TOWNE.

1. I re-mem-ber thee well, I re-member thee well, a sweet lit-tle child, a sweet lit-tle child, So mod-est and gen-
2. O, thy brow is so fair, O, thy brow is so fair, and arched with such grace, and arched with such grace, While crowning thy ho-

tie, so mod-est and gen-tie, so love-ly and mild, so love-ly and mild; Thy voice like a harp, thy voice like a harp that
ly, while crowning thy ho-ly and heav-en-ly face! Thy lips, they are like, thy lips they are like a

the breeze, that yields to the breeze, Where the zeph-yrs of spring, where the zeph-yrs of spring stir the bloom on the trees,
the sun, a rose in the sun, And thy soft cunning laugh, and thy soft cun-ning laugh is a mag-ic-al one,

A SWEET LITTLE CHILD. Concluded.

THE GOLDEN RULE.

F. W. ROOT.

THE CHEERFUL DAY. Round in four parts.

COME AND REST. (Trio for Female voices.)

C. M. WYMAN.

1. Come and rest ye wea - ry, Come where hap-py voic-es greet While the even-ing shades sur-round you, Rest, rest, rest and be your

2. Now no care an - noy - ing, Sounds of toil all hush'd and still La - bor's sweet re-ward en - joy - ing Sleep, sleep, sleep and fear no

slumber sweet, Rest, rest, rest and be your slumber sweet, Rest, rest.

coming Ill, Sleep, sleep, sleep and fear no coming Ill, Sleep, sleep.

SERENADE.

Words by Miss A. D. EDWARDS.

Music by O. D. ADAMS.

1. Sleep, dear - est, sleep! The sil-ver moon is shin - ing—

2. Sleep, dear - est, sleep! The world at peace is ly - ing—

O - ver the throbbing sea, The beating, and pas - sion-ate sea, Her vir - gin brow in - clin - ing, As I in - cline o'er thee! sleep! sleep!

On - ly the nightwinds free, The pas-sion-ate nightwinds so free, Around thy door are sigh - ing, As now I sigh for thee! sleep! sleep!

THE HAPPY FARMER.

From the "Coronet."

1. My song I sing at early dawn of day, As forth to la - bor in the fields I take my way;
2. Be - fore the shades of eve begin to fall I turn toward the cottage 'neath the elm trees tall; And

My song I sing at dawn of day, of day, As to the fields I take my way, my way;
Be - fore the shades be - gin to fall, to fall, I turn, I turn beneath the elm trees tall,

My song I sing at dawn of day, of day, As to the fields I take my way, my way;
Be - fore the shades be - gin to fall, to fall, I turn, I turn beneath the elm trees tall,

brush the dew from many a sparkling flower, And breathe the od - ors sweet from every woodland bower;
liv - ing ech - oes greet my joy - ful song, As gai - ly there I mingle in the household throng.

I brush the dew from many a sparkling flower, And breathe - from ev - ery woodland bower.
And hark echoes, they greet my song, my song, As there I'm with the household throng.

I brush the dew from many a sparkling flower, And breathe from ev - ery woodland bower.
And hark! echoes, they greet my song, my song, As there I'm with the household throng.

THE HAPPY FARMER.—Concluded.

LAUGHING SONG.—Concluded.

SHEPHERD'S SONG.
(In Da Capo sing first verse each time.)

Music from Kreutzer's "Night in Grenada." Arr. by F. W. Ro vt.
Words by J. R. Murray.

1. Down from the loft - y mountains, Where all the day we roam, We hast-en to the fountains, And

2. We come all free from sor - row, With lightsome hearts and gay, And we shall taste to - mor - row, What

pleas - ant vales of home; Our cheerful song is ring - ing, No care nor fear we know; The hills send back our singing In

we en - joy to-day: For sim - ple joys are last - ing, And simple pleasures true, No shad-ow o - ver-casting, To

After Da Capo go from here to Coda.

ech - oes soft and low, The hills send back our singing, In ech - oes soft and low: In humble ways and sweet content, Our

make us sigh for new, No shad - ow o - ver-cast -ing To make us sigh for new: And to our hearts may nev - er come, The

SHEPHERD'S SONG.—Concluded.

peace - ful shep-herd lives are spent, Our flocks se - cure we keep, Our flocks se - cure we keep.

great world's noise and bus - y hum, But peace and qui - et rest, But peace and qui - et rest.

SOPRANO SOLO.

O bet - ter than the

And when the sun - set

DA CAPO.

splendor That shines in all that gold can bring, Are all the joys, Are the joys we sing, we sing, we sing...............

golden, It's brightest glories o'er us fling, Our song we sing, Ah! our song we sing, we sing, we sing...............

CODA.

In ech - oes soft and low,   The hills send back our mer - ry song, In ech - oes soft and low.

In ech - oes soft and low, In ech-oes soft and low, The hills send back our mer - ry song, In ech - oes soft and low.

THE CONTEST.

G. F. ROOT.
From "Sabbath Bell."

O no, join ours, no, ours, O no, join ours, join

Which side shall we join, Which side shall we join? which side? Which side shall we join? Which side shall we

join ours, of course, Oh, this This is the side you should join, you should

ours, join ours, Now you'd really better come with us, with us, Come, come, come,

Join, shall we join? which side? Let us all sing to-geth-er, Let us

Join, you should join, O, the ten-or are so grasping, They would leave us none at all,

THE CONTEST.—Concluded.

LOUD THE STORM IS ROARING.—Concluded.

1st time.

rag-ing o'er us, We will gai - ly laugh and sing, Ha, ha, ha, we'll laugh, ha, ha, ha, and sing, We will laugh and sing. Thus tho'

rag - ing o'er us, We will laugh and sing, laugh and sing. Thus tho'

2d time. FASTER.

sing La, la, tra, la, la, la, la, la, la, la, la, tra, la, la, la, la, la, la, la; Yes, we'll sing, yes, we'll sing, We'll laugh and sing.

sing Tra, la, la, la, la, la, la, tra, la, la, la, la, la, la, la, la, la, la; Yes, we'll sing, yes, we'll sing, We'll laugh and sing.

FASTER.

sing Tra, la, la, la, la, tra, la, la, la, la, tra, la, la, la, la, tra, la, la, la, la; Yes, we'll sing, yes, we'll sing, we'll laugh and sing.

sing La, la, &c.

COME, FOLLOW ME. (Round in Three Parts.)

From the "Musical Album."

Come, fol - low, fol - low, fol - low, fol - low, fol - low, fol - low me. Whith - er sh ll I fol - low, fol - low, fol - low?

Whith - er shall I fol - low, fol - low thee? To the green-wood, to the green-wood, to the green-wood, green-wood tree.

O, SUMMER NIGHT.—Concluded.

CHICAGO STREET-CRIES. (Round, in Six Parts.)

P. P. Bliss.

End with the second measure, when you are ready.
Allegretto.

1. Hark to the street-cries in the nois-y cit-y! Loud-er and loud-er they fall up-on the ear. "Right this

2. way, Sir,' 'Take a carriage?' 'Apples, peanuts, cakes and pies!' 'Oh, here's your nice sweet or-ang-es!' 'The Adams House close by!' 'Bring out your

3. ole clo!' 'Here's your fresh fish!' 'Fire! Fire! Fire!'

4. 'Trib - e - une— Times, Eve - nine Jine - '1— five - o - clock - ng!' 'Straw - ber - ry!'

5. 'P'lice! P'lice! P'lice! P'lice!' 'Bur - ling - ton an' Quin - cy cars!' 'Auc - tion! auc - tion!' 'Milk be - low!'

6. 'Can you tell me, Sir, when the ten - o - clock train goes?' 'Mis - ter, black your boots?' 'O, I've lost my watch!' 'Hurry up!'

COMIN' THRO' THE RYE. (Newly Set.)

If a bod - y meet a bod - y com - in' thro' the rye, If a bod - y kiss a bod - y, need a bod - y cry.
Ev - 'ry las - sie has her lad - die, none they say have I, Yet the lads all smile at me when com - in' thro' the rye.

LOUD THE STORM IS ROARING. (New Words.)

From "Crispino e la Comare," by Ricci.

Arr. by F. W. Root.

Loud the storm is roar - ing Down the tor-rents pour-ing ; Join we now the cho - rus, Tho' dark - ness is o'er us.

Thun-ders crash a - bove us, Still from hearts that love us Comes the sweet song of hope, The sweet song of hope and joy.

Sweet - er seem the bird songs, When storm blasts are 'o - ver ; Bright-er dawns the spring-time, When Win-ter drear is past.

LOUD THE STORM IS ROARING.—Continued.

All our fan-cied sor - row, Turn'd to joy to - mor - row, Will but give great-er joy, Will give great-er joy at last.

All our fan-cied sor-row, Turn'd to joy to-mor-row, Will but give great-er joy, Will give great-er joy at last.

Still the sun in beau - ty Bright is shin - ing, Tho' the clouds in dark - ness Hide their sil - ver lin - ing.

Still the sun in beau-ty Bright is shin - ing, in dark-ness hide their lin-ing.

And tho' for-tune send thee No bright ray, Hope her light will lend thee All the wea-ry way. last. Thus tho' storms are wild-ly

And tho' for-tune send thee No bright ray, Hope her light will lend thee All the wea-ry way. last. Thus tho' storms are wild-ly

LOUD THE STORM IS ROARING.—Concluded.

rag - ing o'er us, We will gai - ly laugh and sing, Ha, ha, ha, we'll laugh, ha, ha, ha, and sing, We will laugh and sing. Thus tho'

rag - ing o'er us, We will laugh and sing, laugh and sing. Thus tho'

sing La, la, tra, la, la, la, la, la, la, la, la, tra, la, la, la, la, la, la; Yes, we'll sing, yes, we'll sing, We'll laugh and sing.

sing Tra, la, la, la, la, la, la, tra, la, la, la, la, la, la, la, la, la, la; Yes, we'll sing, yes, we'll sing, We'll laugh and sing.

sing Tra, la, la, la, la, tra, la, la, la, la, tra, la, la, la, la, tra, la, la, la, la; Yes, we'll sing, yes, we'll sing, we'll laugh and sing.

sing La, la, &c.

COME, FOLLOW ME. (Round in Three Parts.) From the "MUSICAL ALBUM."

Come, fol - low, fol - low, fol - low, fol - low, fol - low, fol - low me. Whith - er sh ll I fol - low, fol - low, fol - low?

Whith - er shall I fol - low, fol - low thee? To the green-wood, to the green-wood, to the green-wood, green-wood too.

WELCOME TO MAY. (Round, in Four Parts.)

Hail to the month, to the cheer-ing month of May. Now to the woods, to the leaf-y woods a-way.

Hear the mer-ry war-blers, the war-blers on the spray; We will all be as hap-py, yes, as hap-py as they.

AH! HOW, SOPHIA.

Arranged from a celebrated Round by Dr. CALLCOTT.

Ah! how, So-phi-a, can you leave, can you leave Your lov-er, your lov-er, and of hope be-reave!

Go fetch the In-dian's bor-row'd plume, bor-row'd plume; Yet rich-er, Yet rich-er far than that your bloom:

I'm but a lodg-er in her heart, in her heart; And more than me, and more than me, I fear, have

Go, go, go, go fetch the In-dian's, fetch the'In-dian's, fetch the In-dian's, fetch the In-dian's, Go fetch the In-dian's Go fetch the

Go, go, go, go, Go, go, go, go, Go fetch the In-dian's, Go fetch the

Ah! how, So-phia, Ah! how, So-phia, Ah! how, So-phia, Ah! how, So-phia, phia, phia, Ah! how, So-phia, phia,

part;   I'm but a lodg-er,   I'm but a lodg-er,   I'm but a

AH! HOW, SOPHIA.—Concluded.

NOT A TEAR, NOT A FEAR. *(New Words.)*   *From " The Huguenots."*   *Arr. by* F. W. ROOT.

1. Not a tear—not a fear At the bugle's sounding, Haste away,—no delay, Soldiers brave and true ; Sabres clash—helmets flash,

D.C. Not a tear—not a fear At the bugle's sounding, Haste away,—no delay, Soldiers brave and true ; Sabres clash—helmets flash,

2. Hear the drum, see them come, Shall we falter ? Never ! Wrong must fail—Right prevail, Raise our banners high : Hear the shout, ringing out,

Every heart is bounding, Comes the call, " Forward all," Dearest love, adieu ! Forward now, on our captain's word re - ly - ing,

Every heart is bounding, Comes the call, " Forward all," Dearest love, adieu !

Lib - er - ty for - ev - er, Firmly stand, sword in hand, Bound to do or die." Forward now, on our captain's word re - ly - ing,

NOT A TEAR, NOT A FEAR.—Concluded.

Forward now, All our country's foes de - fy - ing, Loudly now, Hear the Battle Cry resound, Yes, loud..... hear the Battle Cry, The

Forward now, All our country's foes de - fy - ing, Loudly now, Hear the Battle Cry resound, Yes, loud.... hear the Battle Cry, The

Battle Cry resound! Onward, onward, On to fame and glory, Onward, onward, on to fame and glory glo - ry.

Battle Cry resound! Onward, onward, On to fame and glory, Onward, onward, on to fame and glory, glo - - - - ry.

ADVANCED COURSE.

THE FOREST FESTIVAL.

Words by J. R. MURRAY.
Music Arr. from Offenbach's "Orpheus" by F. W. ROOT.

Allegro leggiero.

1. Sweetest pleasure without measure, Greets us in the woods to-day, As we haste with dear com-pan-ions, From the noi-sy town a-way, Where

2. Kind-ly gleaming, bright eyes beaming, Merry hearts and friendly smiles, Wait us in the woodland now, Where beau-ty ev-ery heart beguiles, Where

brooklets flowing, zeph-yrs blowing, Sing-ing birds in branch-es high, All in-vite us, and de-light us, Giv-ing joy we can-not buy.

ber-ries fair and flow-ers rare, Shall give us roy-al feast to-day, Hearts are light and fac-es bright As to the woods we haste a-way.

yes! yes! Hap-pi-ness is ours to-day; Come! come! come! come! To the woods a-way! a-way! Yes! yes! yes! yes! Hap-pi-ness is

Yes! yes! Hap-pi-ness is ours to-day; Come! come! come! come! To the woods a-way! a-way! Yes! yes! yes! yes! Hap-pi-ness is

THE FOREST FESTIVAL.—Concluded.

THE FUNERAL BELL.—Concluded.

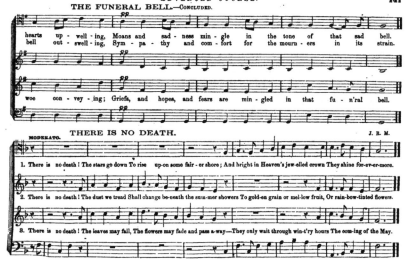

hearts up - well - ing, Moans and sad - ness min - gle in the tone of that sad bell.
bell out - swell - ing, Sym - pa - thy and com - fort for the mourn - ers in its strain.

woe con - vey - ing; Griefs, and hopes, and fears are min - gled in that fu - n'ral bell.

THERE IS NO DEATH.

MODERATO.   J. R. M.

1. There is no death! The stars go down To rise up-on some fair - er shore; And bright in Heaven's jew-elled crown They shine for-ev-er-more.

2. There is no death! The dust we tread Shall change be-neath the sum-mer showers To gold-en grain or mel-low fruit, Or rain-bow-tinted flowers.

3. There is no death! The leaves may fall, The flowers may fade and pass a-way—They only wait through win-t'ry hours The com-ing of the May.

THE UNION BATTLE MARCH.—Concluded.

THE MOUNTAIN MINERS' SONG. *(New Words.)*

Arranged from "Offenbach" by F. W. Root.

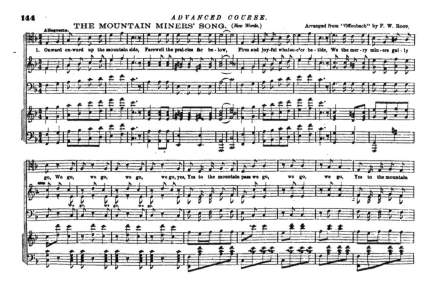

1. Onward on-ward up the mountain side, Farewell the prai-ries far be - low, Firm and joy-ful whatso-e'er be - tide, We the mer - ry min-ers gal - ly

go, We go, we go, we go, we go, yes, Yes to the mountain pass we go, we go, we go, Yes to the mountain

THE MOUNTAIN MINERS' SONG.—Continued.

THE MOUNTAIN MINERS' SONG.—Continued.

MOUNTAIN MINERS' SONG.—Concluded.

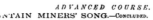

still for the 'gold is there we know,   we know,   we know, on,   move on,   move   on,   move   on   to the
to the mountain pass, to the mountain pass, to the mountain pass, to the mountain

Faster.   Accellerate.

pass we merry miners gaily go, we merry miners gai-ly go, we go, we go, we go, we go......

ELIJAH AND I.

BASE SOLO.

P. P. Bliss.

1. The house that you see un - der - neath the great pine, With walls that are paint - ed and
2. There on the side - hill of the wood - land close by, In a house that is not half so
3. 'Tis good in his blue eyes the twin - kle to see, That the mill may go wrong nev - er
4. He laughs when I frown, and he hums when I sigh The pleas - ant love dit - ties of

VOCAL ACCOMPANIMENT.

La, la, la, la, la, la, la, la, la, &c.

La, la, la, la, la, la, la, la, la, la, &c.

La, la, la, la, la, la, la, la, la, &c.

La, la, la, la, la, la, la, &c.

doors that are fine, And mead - ows and corn - fields a - round it are mine, And mead - ows and corn - fields a - round it are mine.
wide or so high E - li - jah, my mil - ler, lives, *rich - er* than I, E - li - jah, my mil - ler, lives, *rich - er* than I.
troub - les his glee; 'Tis I that must pay for the mend - ing, not he, 'Tis I that must pay for the mend - ing, not he.
days that are by; Now who is the rich - er, E - li - jah or I? Now who is the rich - er, E - li - jah or I?

FAREWELL MY MOUNTAIN HOME.

For Men's Voices.

H. S. SARONI.

ewell my mountain home, Farewell my mountain home, Farewell my mountain home, Farewell my mountain home, Farewell, fare-
ewell my boyhood's dream, Farewell my boyhood's dream, Farewell my boyhood's dream, Farewell my boyhood's dream, Farewell, fare-

SOLO.   CHORUS.   SOLO.   CHORUS.

rewell my mountain home, Farewell my mountain home, Farewell my mountain home, Farewell my mountain home, Farewell, fare-
ewell my boyhood's dream, Farewell my boyhood's dream, Farewell my boyhood's dream, Farewell my boyhood's dream, Farewell, fare-

y mountain home; With si - lent tears I part, I leave a - mid your pur - ple groves The sun-shine of my heart. The
ay boyhood's dream; The hopes of oth - er years A - las, the heart can on - ly woo Its mem - o - ries in tears. Yet

well my mountain home; With si - lent tears I part, I leave a - mid your pur - ple groves The sun-shine of my heart. The
well my boyhood's dream; The hopes of oth - er years A - las, the heart can on - ly woo Its mem - o - ries in tears. Yet

FAREWELL MY MOUNTAIN HOME.—Concluded.

Sum-mer dawn for me no more Will flood the joy-ous hills, No more for me will sing at eve The mer-ry, laughing rills. A-

turn I still a-gain to view The hills I lov'd to roam, And sad-ly bid a fond a-dieu, A-dieu my na-tive home. A-

dieu, a-dieu, my moun-tain home, My own dear mountain home; No more for me will sing at eve The mer-ry, laughing rills.

dieu, a-dieu, my moun-tain home, A-dieu my mountain home; And sad-ly bid a fond a-dieu, A-dieu my na-tive home.

ADVANCED COURSE

RING, RING THE MERRY BELLS.

From the "Coronet." Arr. by G. z.

Ring, ring the mer-ry bells from ev-'ry tow'r,   High in the air. Come, come ye hap-py ones

Ring, ring the mer-ry bells from ev-'ry tow'r, Let the star-ry ban-ner float   in the air. Come, come ye hap-py ones

FINE.

from near and far,   To the brave prepare. Sweet   the   car-ol   of   the   wild birds

from near and far,   Now the joy-ful wel-come to the brave   pre-pare. Sweeter than the car-ol   of the wild birds

RING, RING THE MERRY BELLS.—Continued.

are their · voi-ces as they come, arch-es ring, arch-es ring, With their welcome, with their

are their voi-ces as they come, While the fest-al arch-es ring, While the fes-tal arch-es ring, With their welcome, with their

welcome home! Yes, welcome, welcome home from the war, Honor'd and brave, honor'd and brave! In grateful notes our-voi-ces we pour, To

welcome home! Yes, welcome, welcome home from the war, Honor'd and brave, honor'd and brave! In grateful notes our voi-ces we pour,

RING, RING THE MERRY BELLS.—Concluded.

TUNES, HYMNS, ANTHEMS AND CHANTS.

ADVANCE. L. M.

Triumphantly.

1. TRI-UMPH-ANT Zi-on! lift thy head From dust and dark-ness and the dead; Tho' hum-bled long, a-wake at length, And gird thee with thy Sav - ior's strength

2. Put all thy beau-teous gar-ments on, And let thy va-rious charms be known! Then deck'd in robes of right-eous-ness, The world thy glo-ries shall con - fess.

3. No more shall foes un-clean in - vade, And fill thy hal-low'd walls with dread; No more shall hell's in-sult-ing host Their vic-t'ry and thy sor - rows boast.

ANNABEL. L. M.

Andantino.

1. Sweet is the work, my God, my King, To praise thy name, give thanks, and sing; To show thy love by morn - ing light, And talk of all thy truth at night.

2. Sweet is the day of sa - cred rest; No mor - tal care shall seize my breast: Oh, may my heart in tune be found, Like Da-vid's harp of sol-emn sound!

3. My heart shall tri-umph in my Lord, And bless his works, and bless his word; Thy works of grace, how bright they shine! How deep thy coun-sels, how di-vine!

155

BELLFLOWER. L. M.

1. Bless, O my soul! the liv-ing God; Call home thy tho'ts that rove abroad: Let all the powers with-in me join In work and wor-ship so di-vine.

2. Bless, O my soul! the God of grace His fa-vors claim our high-est praise; Why should the wond-ers he hath wrought Be lost in si-lence, and for-got?

3. Let ev-ery land his power confess; Let all the earth a-dore his grace: My heart and tongue with rap-ture join, In work and wor-ship so di-vine.

BLUE ISLAND. L. M.

1. How pleasant, how di-vine-ly fair, O Lord of hosts, Thy dwellings are! With long desire my spir-it faints, To meet th' assemblies of thy saints, To meet th' assemblies of thy saints.

2. My soul would rest in thine a-bode; My panting heart cries out for God: My God! my King! why should I be So far from all my joys and Thee, So far from all my joys and Thee.

BLEST TIE. L. M.

1. How blest the sa-cred tie that binds, In un-ion sweet, ac-cording minds! How swift the heavenly course they run, Whose heart and faith and hopes are one.

2. To each the soul of each how dear! What jeal-ous care, what ho-ly fear! How doth the gen'rous flame within, Re-fine from earth and cleanse from sin!

CASTELLAN. L. M.

Moderato.

New Hymn.

1. "To die is gain," if burning woe No long-er makes the tear-drops flow; And all the pain of world like this Is swal-low'd in a sea of bliss.
2. "To die is gain," if hope can shed Her ra-diance round the dy - ing bed; If faith can lift the clos - ing eye, To view the glo-ries of the sky.

3. "To die is gain," if cru - el death Is con-quer'd by the dy - ing breath; And we, all vic-tor-crown'd,can sing, "O death, where is thy ven-om sting?"
4. "To die is gain," if Christ is nigh, And we on wings of faith can fly To heav'n a-bove, where an-gels wait, To ope for us the shin - ing gate.

CONTENT. L. M.

Moderato.

From BRICCIALDI, *by J. R.* MURRAY.

1. O Lord, how full of sweet con-tent Our years of pil-grim - age are spent! Where'er we dwell, we dwell with thee, In heav'n, in earth, or on the sea.

2. To us re-main nor place nor time; Our coun-try is in ev - 'ry clime: We can be calm and free from care On an - y shore, since God is there.

CLUSTER. L. M.

Andantino.

1. Soon may the last glad song a - rise Thro' all the mil-lions of the skies—That song of tri-umph which re-cords That all the earth is now the Lord's.

2. Let thrones and pow'rs and king-doms be O - be-dient, might-y God, to thee! And, o - ver land and stream and main, Wave thou the scep-tre of thy reign!

DIADEM. L. M.

1. The Lord how won-drous are His ways! How firm His truth, how large His grace! He takes His mer-cy for His throne, And thence He makes His glo-ries known.

2. Not half so high His power hath spread, The starry heavens a-bove our head, As His rich love ex-ceeds our praise, Ex-ceeds the high - est hopes we raise.

3. Not half so far has na-ture placed The ris - ing morn-ing from the west, As His for-giv - ing grace re-moves, The dai - ly guilt of those He loves.

DE VERE. L. M.

1. Thy hap-py ones a strain be-gin; Dost thou not, Lord, glad souls pos-sess? Thy cheer-ful Spirit dwells with-in ; We feel Thee in our joy-ful-ness.

2. Our mirth is not a-fraid of Thee; Our life re - joic-es to be bright ; We would not from our glad-ness flee, But give full wel-come to de-light.

3. We turn to Thee a smil - ing face, Thou send-est us the smile a-gain ; Our joy, the rich-ness of Thy grace, Thine own, the cheer of this glad strain.

FREELAND. L. M.

Moderato.

1. Now to the Lord a noble song, Awake, my soul, awake my tongue ! Ho-san-na to th' eternal Name, And all His boundless love proclaim !

2. Grace ! 'tis a sweet a charming theme; My tho'ts rejoice at Jesus' name ; Ye angels, dwell upon the sound ; Ye heavens, reflect it to the ground !

3. Oh, may I live to reach the place Where He unveils His lovely face ! Where I His beauties shall behold, And sing His name to harps of gold.

GRAND VISION. L. M.

Recitando.

1. God is the refuge of His saints, When storms of sharp distress invade ; Ere we can offer our complaints, Behold Him present with His aid.

2. Let mountains from their seats be hurled Down to the deep and buried there, Convulsions shake the solid world ; Our faith shall never yield to fear.

HAWTHORNDELL. L. M.

Impressively.

Lo God is here ! let us a - dore, And own how dreadful is this place ! Let all with - in us feel His power, And silent bow be-fore His face !

11

MURRAY'S CHANT. L. M.

P. P. BLISS.

1. Oh, render thanks to God a-bove, The fountain of e - ter - nal love; Whose mercy firm, thro' ages past, Hath stood, and shall forever last.

2. Who can His might-y deeds express—Not on-ly vast, but num-ber-less! What mortal el - o-quence can raise His tribute of im - mor-tal praise.

3. Ex-tend to me that fa-vor, Lord, Thou to thy chosen dost af-ford; When thou return'st to set them free, Let thy salvation vis - it me.

MIRABELLE. L. M.

Con Spirito.   *It will be observed that there are three kinds of time in this tune.*

1. A - wake my soul! lift up thine eyes; See where thy foes a-gainst thee rise, In long ar - ray, a numerous host; A-wake, my soul, or thou art lost!

2. Thou tread'st upon en-chant-ed ground; Perils and snares be - set thee round; Be - ware of all; guard ev'-ry part; But most the trai-tor in thy heart.

3. Come then, my soul! now learn to wield The weight of thine immortal shield; Put on the ar - mor from a - bove, Of heav'n-ly truth, and heav'nly love.

MYRON. L. M.   C. M. WYMAN.

1. O for a sweet, in-spir-ing ray, To an-i-mate our fee-ble strains, From the bright realms of end-less day, The bliss-ful realms where Je-sus reigns.

2. Im-mor-tal glo-ries crown his head, While tune-ful hal-le-lu-jahs rise, And love, and joy and tri-umph spread Thro' all th' as-sem-blies of the skies.

3. He smiles, and ser-aphs tune their songs To bound-less rap-ture, while they gaze; Ten thou-sand thou-sand joy-ful tongues Re-sound his ev-er-last-ing praise.

MINNEISKA. L. M.   F. W. ROOT, 1859.

Moderate.

1. Come, wea-ry souls, with sin dis-tress'd, Come, and ac-cept the prom-is'd rest; The Sav-ior's gra-cious call o-bey, And cast your gloom-y fears a-way.

2. Here mer-cy's bound-less o-cean flows, To cleanse your guilt and heal your woes; Par-don, and life, and end-less peace, How rich the gift! how free the grace!

3. Dear Sav-ior, let thy pow'r-ful love Con-firm our faith, our fears re-move; O, sweet-ly reign in ev-'ry breast, And guide us to e-ter-nal rest.

MAROAN SEA. L. M.

Sostenuto.

1. The bil-lows swell, the winds are high; Clouds o-ver-cast my win-t'ry sky; Out of the depths to Thee I call; My fears are great, my strength is small.

2. A-mid the roar-ing of the sea, My soul still hangs her hopes on Thee; Thy con-stant love, thy faith-ful care, Is all that saves me from de-spair.

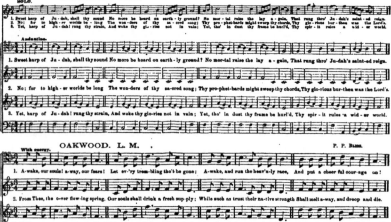

OLEANDER. L. M.

1. Sweet harp of Ju-dah, shall thy sound No more be heard on earth-ly ground? No mor-tal raise the lay a-gain, That rung thro' Ju-dah's saint-ed reign.
2. No; for to high-er worlds belong The won-ders of thy sa-cred song; Thy pro-phet-bards might sweep thy chords, Thy glo-rious bur-then was the Lord's.
3. Yet, harp of Ju-dah! rung thy strain, And woke thy glo-ries not in vain; Yet, tho' in dust thy frame be hurl'd, Thy spir-it rules a wid-er world.

OAKWOOD. L. M.   P. P. Bliss.

1. A-wake, our souls! a-way, our fears! Let ev-'ry trem-bling tho't be gone; A-wake, and run the heav'n-ly race, And put a cheer-ful cour-age on!
2. From Thee, the o-ver flow-ing spring, Our souls shall drink a fresh sup-ply; While such as trust their na-tive strength Shall melt a-way, and droop and die.
3. Swift as an ea-gle cuts the air We'll mount a-loft to thine a-bode; On wings of love our souls shall fly, Nor tire a-mid the heav'n-ly road!

PLANET. L. M.   T. F. SEWARD.

Moderato.

1. Praise ye the Lord! my heart shall join in work so pleasant, so di - vine: My days of praise shall ne'er be passed, While life and, tho't, and being last.

2. Hap - py the man, whose hopes re - ly On Israel's God: He made the sky And earth and seas, and all their train, And none shall find His promise vain.

3 He loves His saints, He knows them well, But turns the wicked down to hell: Thy God, O Zi - on, ev - er reigns, Praise Him in ev - er - last - ing strains.

PALACE. L. M.

Andantino.

1. Behold a Stranger at the door: He gently knocks, has knocked before; Has waited long, is waiting still, You treat no other friend so ill.

2. Oh, welcome Him, the Prince of Peace! Now make His gentle reign increase! Throw wide the door each willing mind; And be His empire all mankind.

PENNOCK'S PORCH. L. M.

Moderato.

Awake, my soul, and with the sun Thy dai - ly stage of duty run; Shake off dull sloth, and joy-ful rise, To pay thy morning sac - ri - fice.

QUIMBY. L. M. JAMES FLINT.

1. Stand up, my soul! shake off thy fears, And gird the gos - pel ar - mor on; March to the gates of end - less joy, Where Je-sus, thy great Cap-tain's gone.

2. Hell and thy sins re - sist thy course; But hell and sin are van-quished foes: Thy Je-sus nailed them to the cross, And sung the tri - umph when he rose.

ROTHSCHILD. L. M. D. SHRYOCK.

1. Praise ye the Lord; ex - alt his name, While in his ho - ly courts ye wait,—Ye saints, who to his house be - long, Or stand at - tend-ing at his gate.

2. Praise ye the Lord! the Lord is good! To praise his name is sweet em-ploy; Is - rael he chose of old, and still His church is his pe - cu - liar joy.

RUBENSTEIN. L. M.

From every storm-y wind that blows, From ev - ery swell-ing tide of woes, There is a calm, a sure re - treat; 'Tis found before the mercy seat.

RENFREW. L. M.

1. Lift up your heads, ye gates! and wide Your ev - er - last-ing doors dis - play; Ye an-gel guards, like flames di-vide, And give the King of glo - ry sway.

2. Who is this King of glo-ry, who? The Lord, om-nip - o - tent to save; Whose own right arm in vic - to - ry, Led cap-tive Death, and spoiled the grave.

3. Lift up your heads, ye gates! and high Your ev - er - last - ing por-tals heave; Wel-come the King of glo-ry nigh; Him must the heaven of heavens re-ceive.

REMINGTON. L. M.

1. Thus far the Lord has led me on, Thus far His power pro-longs my days; And ev-'ry ev'n-ing shall make known Some fresh me-mo-rial of His grace.

2. I lay my bod - y down to sleep; Peace is the pil-low for my head; While well ap-point-ed an-gels keep Their watch-ful sta-tions round my bed.

3. Thus, when the night of death shall come, My flesh shall rest be-neath the ground, And wait Thy voice to rouse my tomb, With sweet sal-va-tion in the sound.

SEPTEMBER. L. M.

SOLO.

1. 'Tis by the faith of joys to come   We walk thro' des-erts dark as night;   Till we ar-rive at heav'n, our home,   Faith is our guide, and faith our light.
2. The want of sight she well sup-plies;   She makes the pearl-y gates ap-pear;   Far in-to dis-tant worlds she pries,   And brings e-ter-nal glo-ries near.
3. With joy we tread the des-ert thro',   While faith in-spires a heav'n-ly ray,   Tho' li-ons roar, and tem-pests blow,   And rocks and dan-gers fill the way.

Billord.

1. 'Tis by the faith of joys to come We walk thro' des - erts dark as night; Till we ar - rive at heav'n our home, Faith is our guide, and faith our light.

2. The want of sight she well sup-plies; She makes the pearl-y gates ap-pear; Far in - to dis - tant worlds she pries, And brings e - ter - nal glo-ries near.

3. With joy we tread the des-ert thro', While faith in-spires a heav'n-ly ray, Tho' li - ons roar and tem-pests blow, And rocks and dan-gers fill the way.

STEADFAST. L. M.

Moderato.

1. Tho' now the na - tions sit be neath The dark-ness of o'er-spread-ing death, God will a - rise with light di - vine, On Zi - on's ho - ly tow'rs to shine.

Light shall glance on dis-tant lands, And hea-then tribes, in joy-ful bands, Come with ex - ult - ing haste to prove The pow'r and great-ness of his love.

2. That Lord, spread the tri - umphs of thy grace; Let truth, and right-eous-ness and peace, In mild and love - ly forms dis-play The glo - ries of the lat - ter day.

TRUVERTON. L. M.
From Schumann by F. W. Root.

Moderato.

1. With all my power of heart and tongue, I'll praise my Maker in my song; An - gels shall hear the notes I raise, Ap - prove the song, and join the praise.

2. To God I cried when troubles rose; He heard me, and subdued my foes: He did my ris - ing fears con-trol, And strength diffused through all my soul.

3. I'll sing thy truth and mer - cy, Lord, I'll sing the wonders of thy word; Not all thy works and names below So much thy power and glo-ry show.

UNION HILL. L. M.
J. E. Gould.

Con Spirito.

1. Wake, O my soul, and hail the morn, For un - to us a Savior's born, See how the an - gels wing their way, To ush - er in the glo - rious day.

2. Hark! what sweet music, what a song, Sounds from the bright ce-les-tial throne; Sweet song whose melting sounds impart Joy to each raptured list'ning heart.

VANDEVERE. L. M.

Gently.

Soft is the light of Sabbath eve, And soft the sunbeams ling'ring there, For these blest hours the world I leave Wafted on wind of faith and prayer.

SAFALA. L. M.

GREATOREX. From "Sabbath Bell" by permission.

Maestoso.

1. Great God of nations! now to thee Our hymn of grat-i-tude we raise; With humble heart, and bending knee, We of-fer thee our songs of praise.

2. Thy name we bless, Almight-y God! For all the kindness thou hast shown To this fair land the pilgrims trod, This land we fond-ly call our own.

3. Great God! preserve us in thy fear, In dangers still our guard-ian be; Oh! spread thy truth's bright precepts here, Let all the peo-ple wor-ship thee.

MURILLO. L. M.

G. F. R. From "Diapason" by permission.

1. Why should we weep for those who die! Those blessed ones who weep no more? Je-sus hath called them to the sky, And glad-ly have they gone be-fore.

2. Far in the distant heavens they shine, But still with borrowed lus-ter glow; Savior, the beams are on-ly thine, Of saints a-bove, or saints be-low.

MELTA. L. M.

Recitando.

G. F. R. From "Sabbath Bell" by permission.

'Tis midnight— ...nd, on Ol-ive's brow, The star is dimm'd that late-ly shone; 'Tis midnight—in the gar-den now The suffering Sav-ior prays a-lone.

SHELTER L. M.

J. Q. W. From "The Coronet" by permission.

Moderato.

1. God is the re-fuge of his saints, When storms of sharp distress in - vade; Ere we can of - fer our complaints, Behold him pres-ent with his aid.

2. Lord may the troubled o - cean roar; In sa-cred peace our souls a - bide; While ev - ery nation, ev - ery shore, Trembles, and dreads the swelling tide.

3. There is a stream, whose gentle flow Supplies the cit - y of our God; Life, love and joy still gliding through, And watering our di-vine a-bode.

DECANDRIA. L. M.

G. F. R. From "The Diapason" by permission.

1. "We've no a - bid-ing cit - y here," This may distress the worldly mind; But should not cost a saint a tear, Who hopes a bet - ter rest to find.

2. "We've no a - bid-ing cit - y here," Sad truth, were this to be our home; But let this thought our spi-rits cheer, "We seek a cit - y yet to come."

LILLIAN. L. M

G. F. R. From "The Sabbath Bell" by permission.

Gently, and not too Fast.

How blest the sacred tie that binds In sweet communion kindred minds! How swift the heavenly course they run, Whose hearts, whose faith, whose hopes are one.

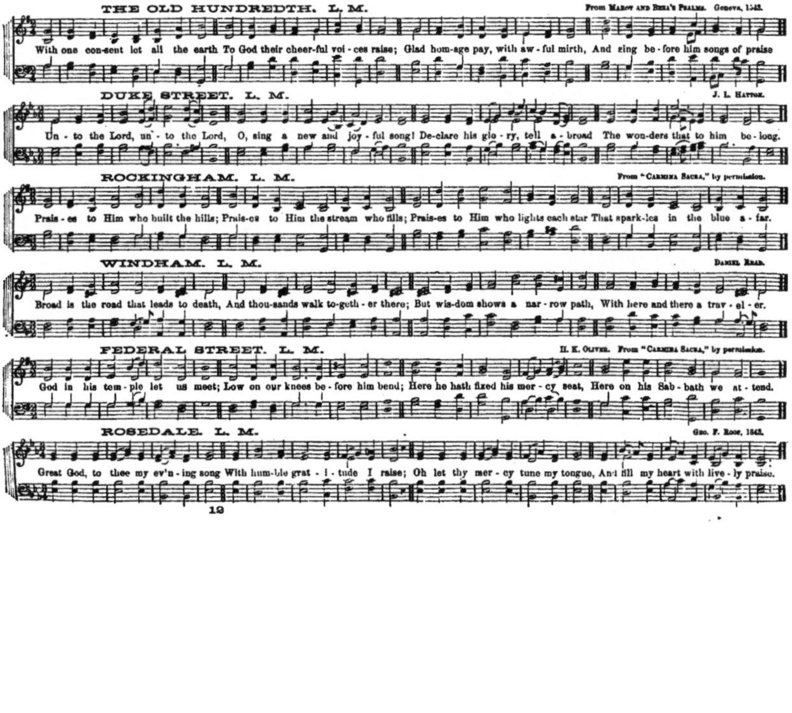
THE OLD HUNDREDTH. L. M.
From Marot and Beza's Psalms. Geneva, 1543.
With one con-sent let all the earth To God their cheer-ful voi - ces raise; Glad hom-age pay, with aw - ful mirth, And sing be - fore him songs of praise
DUKE STREET. L. M.
J. L. Hatton.
Un - to the Lord, un - to the Lord, O, sing a new and joy - ful song! De-clare his glo - ry, tell a - broad The won-ders that to him be - long.
ROCKINGHAM. L. M.
From "Carmina Sacra," by permission.
Prais - es to Him who built the hills; Prais-es to Him the stream who fills; Prais-es to Him who lights each star That spark-les in the blue a - far.
WINDHAM. L. M.
Daniel Read.
Broad is the road that leads to death, And thou-sands walk to-geth - er there; But wis-dom shows a nar - row path, With here and there a trav - el - er.
FEDERAL STREET. L. M.
H. K. Oliver. From "Carmina Sacra," by permission.
God in his tem - ple let us meet; Low on our knees be - fore him bend; Here he hath fixed his mer - cy seat, Here on his Sab - bath we at - tend.
ROSEDALE. L. M.
Geo. F. Root, 1843.
Great God, to thee my ev'n - ing song With hum-ble grat - i - tude I raise; Oh let thy mer - cy tune my tongue, And fill my heart with live - ly praise.

HAMBURG. L. M.   From "Carmina Sacra," by permission.

Thou great In-struct-or, lest I stray, O teach my err - ing feet thy way! Thy truth, with ev - er fresh de-light, Shall guide my doubt-ful steps a-right.

TALLIS' EVENING HYMN. L. M.   Tallis.

Glo - ry to thee, my God, this night, For all the bless-ings of the light; Keep me, O keep me, King of kings, Be-neath thine own al - might - y wings.

MENDON. L. M.

God is our sun, he makes our day; God is our shield, he guards our way; From all as-saults of hell and sin, From foes with out and foes with - in.

STONEFIELD. L. M.   Stanley.

O all ye peo-ple, shout and sing Ho - san - nas to your heav'n-ly King; Where'er the sun's bright glo-ries shine, Ye na-tions, praise His name di-vine.

PARK STREET. L. M.   Venua.

Wake, O my soul, and hail the morn, For un-to us a Savior's born; See, how the angels wing their way, To usher in the glorious day, To usher in the glorious day.

ALL SAINTS. L. M.   W. Knapp.

Who shall as-cend thy heav'n-ly place, Great God, and dwell be-fore thy face? The man who loves re - li - gion now, And hum-bly walks with God be - low.

APOLLO. C. M. *Cheerfully.*

1. How smil-ing wakes the ver - dant year, Ar-rayed in vel - vet green; How glad the cir - cling fields ap-pear, That bound the bloom-ing scene.

2. And hark! from yon me - lo-dious grove, The feath-ered war-blers break, And in - to notes of joy and love, The sol - i - tude a-wake.

3. O let me join th' as-pir - ing lay, That gives my Ma - ker praise; And swell the song more loud than they, And lof - tier prais-es raise.

ANDROS. C. M. *Joyfully.*

1. Oh, praise the Lord! for He is good, In Him we rest ob - tain: His mer-cy has for a-ges stood, And ev-er shall re-main, And ev - er shall re - main.

2. Let all the peo-ple of the Lord, His prais-es spread a - round; Let them His grace and love re-cord, Who have sal-va-tion found, Who have sal-va-tion found.

3. Now let the east in Him re - joice, The west its trib - ute bring, The north and south lift up their voice, In hon-or of their King, In hon-or of their King.

APPENINE. C. M.

With vigor.

1. A-wake, my soul! stretch ev-'ry nerve, And press with vig-or on: A heaven-ly race de-mands thy zeal, A bright, im - mor - tal   crown,   A bright, im-mor-tal crown.

2. A cloud of wit-ness-es a-round Hold thee in full sur-vey;   For-get the steps al - read - y trod,   And on-ward urge thy   way,   And on-ward urge thy way.

3. 'Tis God's all an-i-mat-ing voice, That calls thee from on high; 'Tis His own hand pre-sents the prize, To thine as - pir - ing   eye,   To thine as - pir-ing eye.

BELLEVALE. C. M.

Andantino.

1. Blest be the dear, u - nit-ing love, That will not let us   part: Our bod-ies may far   off re-move; We still are one in heart,   We still are one in heart.

2. Joined in one spir - it to our head, Where He ap-points we go;   We still in Je-sus' foot-steps tread, And show His praise be-low, And show His praise be-low.

3. Par - tak-ers of the Sav-ior's grace, The same in mind and heart,   Not joy, nor grief, nor time, nor place, Nor life, nor death, can part, Nor life, nor death, can part.

BUCKSPORT. C. M.

C. M. WYMAN.

Joyfully.

1. O all ye lands, rejoice in God! Sing praises to His name! Let all the earth with one ac - cord, His wondrous acts proclaim.

2. Tell how the Ho - ly Spir - it's grace Forbids their feet to slide; And as they run the Christian race, Vouchsafes to be their guide.

3. Oh, then, rejoice, and shout for joy, Ye ransomed of the Lord! Be grateful praise your sweet employ, His presence your re - ward.

BOLTON PARK. C. M.

Maestoso.

1. Joy to the world! the Lord is come! Let earth re - ceive her King! Let ev - 'ry heart pre - pare Him room, And heaven and nature sing.

2. Joy to the world! the Savior reigns! Let men their tongues employ, While fields and floods, rocks, hills and plains, Re - peat the sounding joy.

3. He rules the world with truth and grace, And makes the nations prove The glo - ries of His right-eous-ness, And won - ders of His love.

BYLAND'S BAY. C. M.

Impressively.

God moves in a mys - te - rious way, His wonders to perform; He plants His footsteps in the sea, And rides upon the storm, And rides up - on the storm.

CLIO. C. M.

Andantino.

1. My soul how love-ly is the place To which thy God re-sorts! 'Tis heav'n to see his smil-ing face, Tho' in his earth-ly courts.

2. 'Tis there the mon-arch of the skies His sav-ing pow'r displays; And light breaks in up-on our eyes, With kind and quick'ning rays.

3. With his rich gifts the heav'n-ly Dove De-scends and fills the place; While Christ reveals his wondrous love, And sheds a-broad his grace.

CHEYENNE. C. M.

Moderato.

1. Now joy-ful strains we lift on high, A-mid the faith-ful throng Of those who Je-sus mag-ni-fy In sweet and ho-ly song.

2. With an-gel-hosts that dwell a-bove, And weave their gold-en lays A-round the throne of truth and love, We glad ho-san-nas raise.

8. We cel-e-brate the glorious name Of earth's Re-deem-er King; Our tongues a-loud his pow'r proclaim, In heart his grace we sing.

DERRINGFORD. C. M.

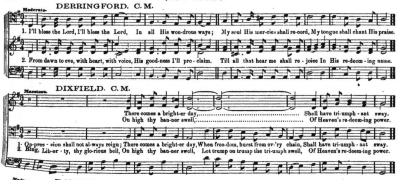

1. I'll bless the Lord, I'll bless the Lord, In all His won-drous ways;   My soul His mer-cies shall re-cord, My tongue shall chant His praise.

2. From dawn to eve, with heart, with voice, His good-ness I'll pro-claim.   Till all that hear me shall re - joice In His re-deem-ing name.

DIXFIELD. C. M.

There comes a bright-er day,.. Shall have tri-umph - ant sway.
On high thy ban-ner swell,.. Of Heaven's re-deem-ing power.

1. Op-pres - sion shall not al-ways reign; There comes a bright-er day, When free-dom, burst from ev-'ry chain, Shall have tri-umph - ant sway.
2. Ring, Lib-er - ty, thy glo-rious bell, On high thy ban-ner swell, Let trump on tramp the tri-umph swell, Of Heaven's re-deem-ing power.

DARROW. C. M.

NEW TUNES.

ERICSON. C. M.

Moderato.

1. I'm not ashamed to own my Lord, Or to de-fend his cause; Mantain the hon-or of his word, The glo-ry of his cross.

2. Je - sus, my God!—I know his name—His name is all my trust; Nor will he put my soul to shame, Nor let my hope be lost.

3. Firm as his throne his promise stands, And he can well se - cure What I've com-mitt - ed to his hands, Till the de - ci - sive hour.

EL PASO. C. M.

Allegretto.

1. A - rise, my soul, my joy - ful power, And triumph in my God; And triumph in my God; A - wake, my voice, and loud proclaim His glorious grace a - broad.

2. The cit - y of my blest a - bode is walled around with grace; Is walled around with grace; Salvation for a bul-wark stands To shield the sa - cred place.

EVAREST. C. M.

Moderato.

Ye hosts of heav'n, ye mighty ones, As-cribe, with one ac - cord, The strength, the power, the majesty, To your al - might-y Lord.

NEW TUNES.

FONTLEROY. C. M.

Moderato.

1. The mercies of my God and King My tongue shall still pursue: Oh, happy, they..................................who, while they sing, These mercies, share them, too.

2. As bright and lasting as the sun, As lofty as the sky, From age to age.................................Thy word shall run, And chance and change defy.

FLOTOW. C. M.

J. R. Murray.

Andantino.

1. To our Redeemer's glorious name Awake the sacred song! O, may His love—im-mor-tal flame, Tune ev-'ry heart and tongue.

2. His love what mortal tho't can reach! What mortal tongue display! Im-ag-i-na-tion's utmost stretch In wonder dies a-way.

GUARDWELL. C. M.

Maestoso.

1. With songs and hon-ors sounding loud, Address the Lord on high: O-ver the heavens He spreads His cloud, And waters veil the sky.

2. He sends His showers of blessings down To cheer the plains be-low; He makes the grass the mountains crown, And corn in valleys grow.

HEATH HILL. C. M. *Andantino.*

1. Soon as I heard my Father say, "Ye children, seek my grace," My heart replied, without de-lay,"I'll seek my Fa-ther's face."

2. Should friends and kindred, near and dear, Leave me to want, or die: My God would make my life his care, And all my need supply.

3. Wait on the Lord, ye trembling saints, And keep your courage up; He'll raise your spirit when it faints, And far exceed your hope.

HAZEL. C. M. Peculiar. *Can be sung to ordinary common metre by repeating third line of words.* *Moderato.*

1. There is an hour of peace-ful rest To mourning wan-d'rers giv'n; There is a joy for souls dis-tress'd, A balm for ev-'ry wounded breast—'Tis found a-bove—in heav'n.

2. There is a home for wea-ry souls, By sin and sor-row driv'n; When toss'd on life's tempest'ous shoals, Where storms a-rise, and o-cean rolls, And all is drear—but heav'n.

3. There, faith lifts up her cheer-ful eye, To bright-er prospects giv'n; And views the tem-pest pass-ing by, The er-ring shadows quickly fly, And all se-rene—in heav'n.

4. There, fragrant flow'rs immortal bloom, And joys supreme are giv'n; There, rays di-vine dis-perse the gloom— Be-yond the confines of the tomb Ap-pears the dawn of heav'n.

IRONVILLE. C. M.

1. To our Redeemer's glorious name A - wake the sa-cred song; Oh, may his love—im-mor - tal flame! Tune ev - 'ry heart and tongue

2. His love, what mortal tho't can reach! What mortal tongue display; Im - ag - i - na-tion's utmost stretch In won - der dies a - way.

3. Dear Lord, while we, a - dor-ing, pay Our hum-ble thanks to thee, May ev' - ry heart with rapture say, "The Sav - ior died for me."

ISRAELLA. C. M.

From Schumann, by F. W. Root.

1. As pants the hart for cooling streams When heated in the chase; So longs my soul, O God, for thee, And thy re-fresh-ing grace.

2. Why rest-less, why cast down, my soul? Trust God; and he'll employ His aid for thee, and change these sighs To thankful hymns of joy.

3. Why rest-less, why cast down, my soul? Hope still; and thou shalt sing The praise of him who is thy God, Thy health's eter - nal spring.

NEW TUNES.

MANITOU. C. M.
Andante.   H. R. Palmer.

1. Thou art the Way: by Thee a-lone, From sin and death we flee; And he who would the Fa-ther seek, Must seek Him, Lord, by Thee

2. Thou art the Truth: Thy word a-lone, True wisdom can im-part; Thou on-ly canst in-form the mind, And pu-ri-fy the heart.

3. Thou art the Life: the rending tomb Proclaims Thy conquering arm; And those who put their trust in Thee, Nor death nor hell shall harm.

4. Thou art the Way, the Truth, the Life, Grant us that Way to know, That Truth to keep, that Life to win, Whose joys e-ter-nal flow.

MILLMONT. C. M.
Moderato.   From Mendelssohn, by F. W. Root.

1. My thoughts surmount these low-er skies, And look with-in the vail; There springs of endless pleasures rise—The waters nev-er fail.

2. Light are the pains that na-ture brings: How short our sorrows are: When with e-ter-nal fu-ture things The present we compare.

3. I would not be a stranger still To that ce-les-tial place, Where I for-ev-er hope to dwell, Near my Redeemer's face.

OGLE COUNTY. C. M.

P. P. Bliss.

Andantino.

1. Oh! could our tho'ts and wish-es fly, A-bove these gloom-y shades, To those bright worlds beyond the sky, Which

Above these gloomy shades, Above these gloom - y shades,
Or reason's feeble ray, Or reason's fee - ble ray,
To guide our upward aim, To guide our up - - ward aim;

2. There joys unseen by mor - tal eyes, Or rea - son's fee - ble ray, In ev - er blooming pros - pect rise, Un-

3. Lord! send a beam of light di - vine To guide our up - ward aim; With one re - vi - ving touch of thine Our

sor - row ne'er in - vades !.

con - scious of de - cay.

lan - guid hearts in - flame.

OLOFF. C. M.

Moderato.

1. While shepherds watch'd their flocks by night, All seat - ed on the ground, The an - gel of the Lord came down, (omit...........) And glo - ry shone a - round.

2. "Fear not," said he, (for mighty dread Had seiz'd their trou - bled mind,) "Glad ti - dings of great joy I bring, (omit...........) To you and all man - kind.

3. "To you, in Da - vid's town, this day, Is born of Da - vid's line, The Savior, who is Christ, the Lord, (omit...........) And this shall be the sign."

18

QUESTWAY. C. M
Andantino.

1. With joy we hail the sa-cred day Which God hath called His own; With joy the summons we o-bey To wor-ship at His throne.

2. Thy chos-en tem-ple, Lord, how fair! Where will-ing votaries throng To breathe the humble, fer-vent prayer, An'l pour the cho-ral song.

3. Great God, we hail the sa-cred day Which Thou hast called Thine own; With joy the summons we o-bey To wor-ship at Thy throne.

ROBERTS. C. M.
Prayerfully.
H. R. PALMER.

1. Be mer-ci-ful to me, O God! Be mer-ci-ful to me; For though I sink be-neath Thy rod, Yet do I trust in Thee.

2. Thou knowest, Lord, my flesh, how frail, Strong tho' my spir-it be; Oh, then as-sist when foes as-sail, The soul that clings to Thee.

REDWING. C. M.
Firmly.
P. P. BLISS.

No change of time shall ev-er shook My trust, O Lord, in Thee; For Thou hast al-ways been my Rock, A sure de-fense to me.

TOLLINGHILL. C. M. 6 lines, *or Double by singing first half twice, for first verse.*

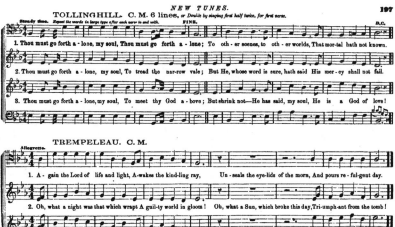

1. Thou must go forth a - lone, my soul, Thou must go forth a - lone; To oth - er scenes, to oth - er worlds, That mor-tal hath not known.

2. Thou must go forth a - lone, my soul, To tread the nar-row vale; But He, whose word is sure, hath said His mer - cy shall not fail.

3. Thou must go forth a - lone, my soul, To meet thy God a - bove; But shrink not—He has said, my soul, He is a God of love!

TREMPELEAU. C. M.

1. A - gain the Lord of life and light, A - wakes the kind-ling ray, Un - seals the eye-lids of the morn, And pours re - ful-gent day.

2. Oh, what a night was that which wrapt A guil-ty world in gloom! Oh, what a Sun, which broke this day, Tri-umph-ant from the tomb!

3. This day be grate-ful hom-age paid, And loud ho-san-nas sung; Let glad-ness dwell in ev - 'ry heart, And praise on ev-'ry tongue.

VINEYARD. C. M.

1. How sweet, how heav'n-ly is the sight, When those who love the Lord In one an-oth-er's peace de-light, And so ful-fil His word.

2. When each can feel his broth-er's sigh, And with him bear a part! When sor-row flows from eye to eye, And joy from heart to heart.

3. When free from en-vy, scorn and pride, Our wish-es all a-bove, Each can his broth-er's fail-ings hide, And show a broth-er's love!

VICAR. C. M.

T. W. HANNUM.

1. When as re-turns this sol-emn day, Man comes to meet his God, What rites, what hon-ors shall he pay, How spread His praise a-broad?

2. From mar-ble domes and gild-ed spires Shall clouds of in-cense rise? And gems, and gold, and gar-lands deck The cost-ly sac-ri-fice.

3. Vain, sin-ful man! cre-a-tion's Lord Thine off'-rings well may spare; But give thy heart, and thou shalt find, Thy God will hear thy prayer.

WILLETT. C. M.

1. When all thy mer - cies, O my God, My ris - ing soul sur - veys, Trans - ported with the view, I'm lost In won - der, love, and praise !

2. When, in the slip - pery paths of youth, With heedless step I ran, Thine arm, unseen, convey'd me safe, And led me up to man.

3. Through all e - ter - ni - ty to thee A joy - ful song I'll raise: But, oh ! e - ter - ni - ty's too short To ut - ter all thy praise.

WARDWAY. C. M.

1. Let ev - ery mor - tal ear at - tend, And ev - ery heart re - joice; The
2. Ho! all ye hun - gry, starv - ing souls, That feed up - on the wind, And

1. Let ev - ery mor - tal ear at - tend, Let ev - ery mor - tal ear at - tend, And ev - ery heart re - joice, And ev - ery heart re - joice; The
2. Ho! all ye hun - gry, starving souls, Ho! all ye hun - gry, starv - ing souls, That feed up - on the wind, That feed up - on the wind, And

trum - pet of strive the gos - pel sounds With an in - vit - ing voice.
rain - ly with earth - ly toys To fill an emp - ty mind.

trum - pet of the gos - pel sounds, The trum - pet of the gos - pel sounds With an in - vit - ing voice, With an in - vit - ing voice.
rain - ly strive with earth - ly toys, And vain - ly strive with earth - ly toys To fill an emp - ty mind, To fill an emp - ty mind.

YARE VALLEY. C. M.

1. Oh, that the Lord would guide my ways To keep His stat-utes still! Oh, that my God would grant me grace To know and do His will!

2. Order my footsteps by Thy word, And make my heart sincere; Let sin have no do-min-ion, Lord, But keep my conscience clear.

3. Make me to walk in Thy commands, 'Tis a de-light-ful road; Nor let my head, nor heart, nor hands Offend a-gainst my God.

YELAM. C. M.

'Tis by Thy strength the mountains stand, God of e-ter-nal power! The sea grows calm at Thy command, And tempests cease to roar.

ZINDA. C. M.   C. M. WYMAN.

1. Fa-ther of mercies God of love, My Father and my God; I'll sing the honors of Thy name, And spread Thy praise abroad.

2. Teach me in time of deep dis-tress, To own Thy hand, O God; And in sub-mis-sive si-lence learn, The lessons of Thy rod.

3. Then may I close my eyes in death, Redeemed from anxious fear; For death it-self, my God, is life, If Thou be with me there

GUIDE. C. M.

Moderato. H. W. J. From the "Coron...

How precious is the book di - vine, By in - spi - ra-tion given! Bright as a lamp its doctrines shine, To guide our souls to heaven.

DEERPATH. C. M.

With Expression. G. F. R. From the "Sabbath Bell," by permission.

I'm not ashamed to own my Lord, Or to de - fend his cause; Maintain the hon - or of his word, The glo - ry of his cross.

BRADFORD. C. M.

Arranged by G. F. R. From the "Shawm," by permission.

I know that my Re - deem - er lives, And ev - er prays for me: A to - ken of his love he gives, A pledge of lib - er - t

SILOAM.* C. M.

From the "Dulcimer,"
By permission of F. J. Huntington, N. Y.

With gentleness. Cres. and Dim. (*May be sung as a Quartett.—The small notes, seldom used, are intended for the flute or some similar instrument.*)

1. By cool Si - lo - am's shad - y rill How fair the lil - ly grows! How sweet the breath, be-neath the hill, Of Sha - ron's dew - y rose.

2. Lo! such the child whose ear - ly feet The paths of peace have trod, Whose se - cret heart, with influence sweet, Is up - ward drawn to God.

GLASGOW. C. M.

Moderato.

G. F. R. From the "Shawm," by permission.

1. A glo - ry gilds the sa - cred page, Ma - jes - tic, like the sun: It gives a light to ev - ery age; It gives, but bor - rows none.

2. The hand that gave it still sup-plies The gra - cious light and heat; Its truths up - on the na - tions rise; They rise, but ne - ver set

3. Let ev - er - last - ing thanks be thine For such a bright dis - play, As makes a world of dark - ness shine With beams of heavenly day.

*The effort was made to obtain some music in Mr. Woodbury's hand-writing, but without success. His many friends will, however, be glad to see attached to one of his most beautiful tunes a fac-simile of his autograph. See pages 338, 339 and 340, for fac-similes of the hand-writing of other prominent musical men.

SPIRES. C. M.

G. F. R. From the "Diapason," by permission.

SOLO, for Soprano Voice.

1. My soul, how love-ly is the place To which thy God re-sorts! 'Tis heav'n to see his smil-ing face, Tho' in his earth-ly courts.

2. There the great Mon-arch of the skies His sav-ing pow'r dis-plays; And light breaks in up-on our eyes With kind and quick 'ning rays.

3. With his rich gifts the heav'n-ly Dove De-scends and fills the place; While Christ re-veals his won-drous love, And sheds a-broad his grace.

VARINA. C. M. Double.

G. F. R. From the "Sabbath Bell," by permission.

Not too fast.

1. There is a land of pure de-light, Where saints im-mor-tal reign; In-fi-nite day ex-cludes the night, And pleas-ures ban-ish pain.

3. Sweet fie'ds be-yond the swell-ing flood, Stand dress'd in liv-ing green; So to the Jews old Ca-naan stood, While Jor-dan roll'd be-tween.

2. There ev-er-last-ing spring a-bides, And nev-er-with-'ring flow'rs; Death, like a nar-row sea, di-vides This heav'n-ly land from ours.

4. But tim-'rous mor-tals start and shrink To cross this nar-row sea; And lin-ger, shiv-'ring on the brink, And fear to launch a-way.

ALMOND. S. M.

Moderato.

1. O where shall rest be found, Rest for the wea - ry soul; 'Twere vain the o - cean's depths to sound, Or pierce to ei - ther pole.

2. The world can nev - er give The bliss for which we sigh; 'Tis not the whole of life to live, Nor all of death to die.

3 Be-yond this vale of tears There is a life a - bove, Un-meas-ured by the flight of years, And all that life is love.

ASHMORE. S. M.

Allegretto.

1. My soul, re-peat His praise, Whose mer-cies are so great; Whose an-ger is so slow to rise, So read-y to a - bate, So read-y to a - bate.

2. His power sub-dues our sins, And His for-giv - ing love, Far as the east is from the west, Doth all our guilt re-move, Doth all our guilt re-move.

3. High as the heav'ns are raised, A-bove the ground we tread, So far the rich-es of His grace, Our high-est tho'ts ex - ceed, Our high-est tho'ts ex-ceed.

14

BARONE. S. M.

Joyfully.

1. How beauteous are their feet, Who stand on Zi-on's hill, Who bring sal-va-tion on their tongues, And words of peace reveal.

2. How charming is their voice! How sweet the tidings are!— "Zi - on, behold thy Sav - ior King! He reigns and triumphs here."

3. How hap-py are our ears, That hear the joy - ful sound, Which kings and prophets wait-ed for, And sought, but nev-er found!

BALLENTINE. S. M.

Moderato.

1. Come, we who love the Lord, And let our joys be known; Join in a song of sweet ac - cord, And thus sur - round the throne.

2. The hill of Zi - on yields A thousand fra - grant sweets, Be-fore we reach the heavenly fields, Or walk the gold - en streets.

3. Then let our songs a-bound, And ev -'ry tear be dry; We're marching thro' Im - man-uel's ground, To fair - er worlds on high.

CLARE, or, Along the Silent Path. S. M. (*New Hymn.*)   F. W. Root.

1. A-long the si - lent path, By count-less spirits trod, An - oth - er wea - ry trav - el - er, Gone up to dwell with God.

2. Gone up from human love, To high - er love and care, From pain be - low to peace a-bove, In man-sions, O so fair.

3. Attune our hearts, O Lord, Tho' they with sorrow swell, To say this meek, submissive word, Thou do - est all things well.

4. Fit us, O Lord, to go, Or fit us here to stay; That we may walk with Thee below, Or up the si - lent way.

CLYMER. S. M.

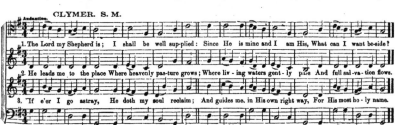

1. The Lord my Shepherd is; I shall be well sup-plied: Since He is mine and I am His, What can I want be-side?

2. He leads me to the place Where heavenly pas-ture grows; Where liv - ing waters gent - ly pass And full sal - va - tion flows.

3. If e'er I go astray, He doth my soul reclaim; And guides me, in His own right way, For His most ho - ly name.

DUCHESS HILL. S. M. Triple, *or Double by repeating first verse as a chorus after each two.*

1. How beauteous are their feet, Who stand on Zi - on's hill! Who bring sal - va - tion on their tongues, And words of peace re - veal.
D.C. How hap - py are our ears, That learn the joy - ful sound, Which kings and prophets waited for, And sought but nev - er found

2. How bless - ed are our eyes, That see this heavenly light! Prophets and kings de - sired it long, But died without the sight.
D.C. The Lord makes bare His arm, Thro' all the earth a - broad : Let ev - 'ry na - tion now be-hold Their Sav - ior and their God.

How charming is their voice! How sweet the tidings are!— "Zi - on, behold thy Savior King! He reigns and triumphs here."

The watchmen join their voice, And tuneful notes em - ploy ; Je - ru - sa - lem breaks forth in songs, And deserts learn the joy.

DEAR HOME. S. M.

T. MARTIN TOWNE.

For - ev - er with the Lord, A - men so let it be ! Life from the dead is in the word, 'Tis im - mor - tal - i - ty.

2. Here in the bod - y pent, Ab-sent from Him I roam; Yet night-ly pitch my mov-ing tent, A day's march near-er home.

EARLY MORN. S. M.

Two kinds of time.

1. Give to the winds thy fears; Hope on, be not dismayed; God hears thy sighs and counts thy tears; God shall lift up thy head.

2. Thro' waves and clouds and storms, He gently clears thy way: Wait thou His time: the dark-est night Shall end in brightest day.

EMELIA. S. M.

Allegretto.

1. Sweet is the work, O Lord, Thy glo-rious acts to sing, To praise Thy name and hear Thy word, And grateful offerings bring.

2. Sweet, at the dawning light, Thy boundless love to tell, And when approach the shades of night. Still on the theme to dwell.

FAIR ISLAND. S. M.   C. M. WYMAN.

Firmly.

1. I stand on Zion's mount, And view my starry crown: No power on earth my faith can shake, Nor hell can thrust me down.

2. The lofty hills and towers,
That lift their heads on high,
Shall all be leveled low in dust—
Their very names shall die.

3. The vaulted heavens shall fall,
Built by Jehovah's hands;
But firmer than the heavens, the Rock
Of my salvation stands.

GOLDEN CITY. S. M.

Cantabile.

1. Come, we who love the Lord, And let our joys be known; Join in a song of sweet ac - cord, And thus sur - round the throne.
2. The hill of Zi - on yields, A thousand sa - cred sweets, Be-fore we reach the heaven - ly fields, Or walk the gold-en streets.
3. Then let our songs a-bound, And ev - ery tear be dry; We're marching through Immanuel's ground, To fair - er worlds on high.

1. Come, we who love the Lord, And let our joys be known; Join in a song of sweet ac - cord, And thus surround the throne.
2. The hill of Zion yields, A thousand sacred sweets, Before we reach the heavenly fields, Or walk the golden streets.
3. Then let our songs abound, And every tear be dry; We're marching through Immanuel's ground, To fairer worlds on high.

1. Come, we who love the Lord, And let our joys be known; Join in a song of sweet ac - cord, And thus sur - round the throne.
2. The hill of Zi - on yields, A thousand sa - cred sweets, Be-fore we reach the heaven - ly fields, Or walk the gold-en streets.
3. Then let our songs a-bound, And ov - ery tear be dry; We're marching through Immanuel's ground, To fair - er worlds on high.

HIAWATHA. C. M.

W. IRVING HARTSHORN.
Ritard.

Gently.

1. One sweet-ly sol - emn thought Comes to me o'er and o'er, Near-er my part-ing hour am I Than e'er I was be-fore.
2. Near-er my Fath - er's house, Where man-y mansions be; Near-er the throne where Je-sus reigns,—Nearer the crys - tal sea;
3. Near-er my go - ing home, Lay-ing my bur-den down, Leaving my cross of heav-y grief, Wear-ing my star - ry crown.

ITHAMER. S. M.

1. A-rise, ye saints a-rise ! The Lord our Lead-er is ; The foe be-fore His ban - ner flies, For vic-to-ry is His.

2. We'll fol-low Thee, our Guide, Our Sav-ior and our King, We'll fol-low Thee, thro' grace sup-plied, From heaven's e-ter-nal Spring.

3. We hope to see the day, When all our toils shall cease; When we shall cast our arms a - way, And dwell in end-less peace.

JERROLD. S. M.

1. We lift our hearts to Thee, Thou Day-star from on high; The sun it-self is but Thy shade, Yet cheers both earth and sky.

2. Oh, let Thy ris-ing beams Dis-pel the shades of night; And let the glo - ries of Thy love, Come like the morn-ing light.

3. How beau-teous na-ture now, How dark and sad be-fore! With joy we view the pleas-ing change, And na-ture's God a - dore.

NEW TUNES.

JULIAN. S. M.   N. D. Coon.

1. While my Re-deem-er's near, My Shep-herd and my Guide, I bid fare-well to anx-ious fear; My wants are all sup-plied.

2. To ev - er fra-grant meads, Where rich a-bun-dance grows, His gra-cious hand in-dul-gent leads, And guards my sweet re-pose.

3. Dear Shep-herd, if I stray, My wan-d'ring feet re - store; To thy fair pas-tures guide my way, And let me rove no more.

JUNALISKA. S. M.

1. What cheer-ing words are these? Their sweet-ness who can tell? In time and to e - ter - nal days, "'Tis with the right-eous well."

2. Well, when they see His face, Or sink a - mid the flood; Well, in af-flic-tion's thorn-y maze, Or on the mount with God.

3. 'Tis well, when joys a - rise; 'Tis well, when sor-rows flow; 'Tis well, when dark-ness vails the skies, And strong temp-ta-tions grow.

KEYESVILLE. S. M.

ed faes a - rise; The hosts of sin are press-ing hard To draw thee from the skies; The hosts of sin are press-ing hard To draw thee from the skies.

KIRTLAND PLACE. S. M.

1. "The Lord is risen indeed:" Now is His work performed; Now is His mighty Captive freed, And death our foe disarmed.

2. "The Lord is risen indeed:" At - tend - ing an - gels, hear: Up to the courts of heaven, with speed, The joy - ful tid - ings bear.

3. Then take your golden lyres, And strike each cheerful chord; Join all the bright ce - les - tial choirs, To sing our ris - en Lord.

LAKE STREET. S. M.

1. Great is the Lord our God, And let His praise be great; He makes His churches His a - bode, His most de-light-ful seat.

2. These temples of His grace— How beau - ti - ful they stand! The honors of our native place, And bulwarks of our land.

3. In Zi - on God is known, A ref - uge in dis - tress; How bright has His sal - va-tion shone Thro' all Her pal - a - ces.

LA GRANGE. S. M.

Oh, cease my wandering soul, On restless wings to roam; All this wide world, to ei - ther pole, Hath not for thee a home.

LONGFELLOW. S. M.

1. My soul, repeat his praise, Whose mercies are so great; Whose anger is so slow to rise, So ready to a - bate.

2. His power subdues our sins, And his for-giv-ing love, Far as the east is from the west, Doth all our guilt re - move.

3. High as the heavens are raised Above the ground we tread, So far the riches of his grace Our highest tho'ts ex - ceed.

4. My soul, repeat his praise, Whose mercies are so great; Whose anger is so slow to rise, So ready to a - bate.

LIGONIER. S. M.

1. Oh, bless the Lord, my soul! Let all with-in me join, And aid my tongue to bless his name, Whose favors are divine.

2. Oh, bless the Lord, my soul! Nor let his mercies lie For-got-ten in un-thankfulness, And without praises die.

3. He crowns thy life with love, When ransomed from the grave; He, who redeemed my soul from hell, Hath sovereign power to save.

MARLAND'S MILLS. S. M.

1. A charge to keep I have, A God to glo-ri-fy; A nev-er dy-ing soul to save, And fit it for the sky.

2. To serve the present age, My call-ing to full-fill;— Oh, may it all my powers engage, To do my Master's will.

MORIAL. S. M. CHARLES HEYER.

1. To praise our Shepherd's care, His wis-dom, love, and might, Your loudest, lof-tiest songs prepare, And bid the world u-nite.
2. Supremely good and great, He tends His blood-bought fold: He stoops, tho' throned in highest state, The feeblest to up-hold.

1. To praise our Shepherd's care, His wisdom, love, and might,...... Your loudest, loftiest songs prepare, And bid them all u-nite.
2. Supremely good and great, He tends His blood bought fold,....... He stoops, tho' throned in high-est state, The feeblest to up-hold.

NORTHERN LIGHT. S. M. C. M. WYMAN.

1. Did Christ o'er sin-ners weep, And shall our cheeks be dry? Let floods of pen-i-ten-tial grief Burst forth from ev-'ry eye.

2. The Son of God in tears The wondering an-gels see! Be thou as-ton-ished, O my soul! He shed those tears for thee.

3. He wept that we might weep: Each sin demands a tear: In Heaven a-lone no sin is found, And weeping is not-there.

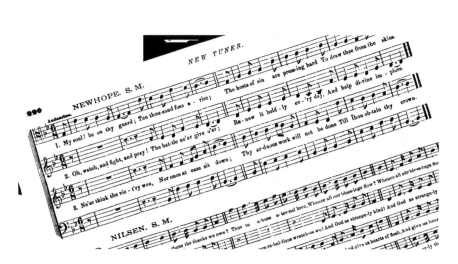

NEW TUNES.

NEWHOPE. S. M.

220

1. My soul! be on thy guard; Ten thou-sand foes a - rise; The hosts of sin are press-ing hard To draw thee from the skies.

2. Oh, watch, and fight, and pray! The bat-tle ne'er give o'er; Re - new it bold - ly ev - 'ry day, And help di-vine im - plore.

3. Ne'er think the vic - t'ry won, Nor once at ease sit down; Thy ar-duous work will not be done Till thou ob-tain thy crown.

NILSEN. S. M.

those the thanks we owe? Thus to a-buse a - ter-nal love, Whence all our bless-ings flow? Whence all our bless-ings flow

more re-bel-lious wretch-es wo! And God as strange-ly kind! And God as strange-ly

nd give us hearts of flesh, And give us hear

rl-y th

NECTARINE. S. M

Andantino.

1. When o‑ver‑whelm'd with grief, My heart with‑in me dies; Help‑less, and far from all re‑lief, To heav'n I lift mine eyes.

2. O, lead me to the Rock That's high a‑bove my head! And make the cov‑ert of thy wings My shel‑ter and my shade.

3. With‑in thy pres‑ence, Lord, For‑ev‑er I'll a‑bide; Thou art the tow'r of my de‑fense, The ref‑uge where I hide.

OPHINETT. S. M.

Moderato.

1. My soul, it is thy God Who calls thee by his grace; Now loose thee from each cum‑b'ring load, And bend thee to the race, And bend thee to the race.

2. Make thy sal‑va‑tion sure, All sloth and slum‑ber shun; Nor dare a mo‑ment rest se‑cure, Till thou the goal hast won, Till thou the goal hast won.

3. Thy crown of life hold fast; Thy heart with cour‑age stay; Nor let one trem‑bling glance be cast A‑long the back‑ward way, A‑long the back‑ward way.

ORLAND'S REST. S. M.

Moderato.   J. R. MURRAY.

1. Send down thy rest, O God! Our toils and tears to crown; Too long the thorn‑y path we've trod; Thy rest, O God, send down; Too long the thorn‑y path we've trod; Thy rest, O God, send down!

2. A liv‑ing faith im‑part Our ques‑tion‑ing to still; With hope in‑spire each faint‑ing heart, And nerve each fal‑t'ring will; With hope in‑spire each faint‑ing heart, And nerve each fal‑t'ring will.

204

NEW TUNES.

RHINELAND. S. M.   CHARLES HEYER.

Andantino

1. The Lord my Shepherd is :...... I shall be well sup-plied: ...... Since He is mine and I am His, What can I want be - side?

2. He leads me to the place, Where heavenly pasture grows: ... Where liv - ing wa - ters gently pass, And full sal - va - tion flows.

3. If e'er I go a - stray. He doth my soul re - claim, And guides me in His own right way, For His most ho - ly name.

SCHUMANN. S. M.   F. W. ROOT, 1869.

Moderato.

1. One sweetly solemn thought Comes to me o'er and o'er Near - er my part-i ig hour am I Than e'er I was be - fore.

2. Near - er my Father's home, Where many man - sions be ; Near - er the throne where Jesus reigns, Nearer the crystal sea.

3. Near - er my Father's home, Lay - ing my bur - den down, Leav - ing my cross of heavy grief, Wearing my starry crown.

TOURJEE. S. M.   P. P. BLISS.

Quietly.

1. Night is the time to rest, How sweet, when labors close, To gather round an aching breast, The curtain of repose.

2. Night is the time to rest, To wet with unseen tears, Those graves of memory where sleeps The joys of other years.

3. Night is the time to pray,
   Our Savior oft withdrew
   To desert mountains far away
   So will His followers do.

4. Night is the time for death,
   When all around is peace,
   Calmly to yield the weary breath,
   From sin and suffering cease.

CROSBY. S. M.

G. F. R. From "The Sabbath Bell," by permission.

Andante.

1. While my Redeemer's near, My Shepherd and my Guide, I bid farewell to ev-'ry fear; My wants are all sup-plied.

2. To ev-er fragrant meads, Where rich abundance grows, His gracious hand in-dul-gent leads, And guards my sweet repose.

SHEPHERD. S. M.

G. F. R. From "The Coronet," by permission.

Andantino.

1. The Lord my Shepherd is; I shall be well supplied; Since He is mine and I am His, What can I want beside!

2. He leads me to the place Where heavenly pasture grows, Where living waters gently pass, And full sal-va-tion flows.

AHIRA S. M.

GREATOREX. From "The Sabbath Bell," by permission.

Behold! the day is come, The righteous Judge is near; And sinners, trembling at their doom, Shall soon their sentence hear.

15

POPULAR TUNES.

EVLEEN. S.M.

Graceful and Flowing.

1. How gentle God's commands! How kind His precepts are! Come, cast your bur - dens on the Lord, And trust...

2. Be - neath His watchful eye His saints se - cure-ly dwell; That hand which bears all na - ture up, Shall guard His children well.

W. B. B. and G. F. R. From the "Diapason," by permission.

WINCHELL. S.M.

1. Oh, where shall rest be found— Rest for the wea - ry soul? 'Twere vain the o - cean depths to sound, Or pierce to ei - ther pole.

2. ...for which we sigh; 'Tis not the whole of life to live, Nor all of death to die.

G. F. R. From the "Diapason," by permission.

...heds His love abroad.

ST. THOMAS. S. M. A. WILLIAMS.

My soul, re - peat His praise, Whose mer-cies are so great; Whose an - ger is so slow to rise, So rea - dy to a - bate.

SHIRLAND. S. M. STANLEY.

How per - fect is Thy word! And all Thy judg-ments just! For ev - er sure thy prom - ise, Lord, And we se - cure - ly trust.

SILVER STREET. S. M. I. SMITH.

Come, sound his praise a - broad, And hymns of glo - ry sing; Je - ho - vah is the sov 'reign God, The un - i - ver - sal King.

THATCHER. S. M. HANDEL.

To God, in whom I trust, I lift my heart and voice; O, let me not be put to shame, Nor let my foes re - joice.

PLYMOUTH. S. M. Old American Melody.

With hum - ble heart and tongue, My God, to thee I pray; O, bring me now, while I am young, To thee, the liv - ing way.

MORNINGTON. S. M. MORNINGTON.

To bless Thy chos - en race, In mer - cy, Lord, in - cline: And cause the bright ness of Thy face On all Thy saints to shine.

ANAMOSA. 7s.

BANDLINE. 7s.

EYTINGE. 7s.

1. Praise the Lord, his glo-ries show, Saints with-in his courts be-low, An-gels round his throne a-bove, All that see and share his love!

2. Earth to heaven, and heaven to earth, Tell his won-ders, sing his worth; Age to age, and shore to shore, Praise him, praise him ev-er-more!

3. Strings and voices, hands and hearts, In the con-cert bear your parts; All that breathe, your Lord a-dore; Praise him, praise him ev-er-more!

FONTAINE. 7s.

1. "Come up hither; come a-way;" Thus the ransomed spir-its sing; Here is cloud-less, end-less day; Here is ev-er-last-ing spring.

2. Come up hither; come and dwell With the liv-ing hosts a-bove; Come, and let your bo-soms swell With their burn-ing songs of love.

3. Come up hither; come and share All the sa-cred joys that rise, Like an o-cean, ev-er-y-where Through the myr-iads of the skies.

FREESTONE. 7 s.

1. Songs of praise the an-gels sang, Heav'n with hal-le - lu - jahs rang, When Je - ho-vah's work be - gun, When he spake, and it was done.

2. Songs of praise a - woke the morn, When the Prince of Peace was born: Songs of praise a - rose when he Cap-tive led cap - tiv - i - ty.

3. Saints be - low, with heart and voice, Still in songs of praise re-joice; Learning here, by faith and love, Songs of praise to sing a - bove.

GOING HOME. 7 s.   THEO. T. CRANE.

1. Soft - ly, now, the light of day Fades up - on my sight a - way; Free from care, from la-bor free, Lord! I would commune with Thee.

2. Soon for me, the light of day Shall for - ev - er pass a - way; Then, from sin and sorrow free, Take me, Lord, to dwell with Thee.

HORIZON. 7s, 6 lines.

1. Glo - ry, glo - ry to our King! Crowns unfading wreathe His head; Je - sus is the name we sing— Je - sus ris - en from the dead;
D.C. Je - sus, Conqu'ror o'er the grave, Je - sus, mighty now to save.

2. Now behold Him high enthroned, Glo-ry beaming from His face! By a - dor - ing an - gels owned, God of ho - li - ness and grace!
D.C. Oh, for hearts and tongues to sing, "Glo-ry, glo - ry to our King!"

IMPERIAL. 7s, Double.   C. M. WYMAN.

1. Songs of praise the an - gels sang, Heaven with hal-le - lu - jah's rang, When Je - ho-vah's work be - gun, When He spake and it was done.

2. Saints be - low with heart and voice, Still in songs of praise rejoice, Learning here by faith and love, Songs of praise to sing a - bove;

Songs of praise awoke the morn, When the Prince of Peace was born; Songs of praise a-rose when He, Cap - tive led cap - tiv - i - ty.

Borne up - on their lat - est breath, Songs of praise shall conquer death; Then amid e - ter - nal joy, Songs of praise their powers employ.

DANBURY. 7s. G. F. R. From the "Diapason," by permission.

Reverentially.

Hark, my soul! it is the Lord; 'Tis thy Savior, hear his word; Jesus speaks, and speaks to thee: "Say, poor sinner, lov'st thou me;'

BIGELOW. 7s. 6 lines. G. F. R. From the "Shawm," by permission.

Allegretto.

{ Christ, whose glo - ry fills the sky, Christ, the true, the on - ly light, } Day spring from on high, be near; Day - star, in my heart ap - pear!
{ Sun of Right-eous-ness! a - rise ; Triumph o'er the shades of night; }

IVES. 7s. Double. E. Ives.

Allegretto.

Who are these in bright array, This ex - ult - ing, happy throng, Round the altar, night and day, Hymning one triumphant song?

"Worthy is the Lamb, once slain, Blessing, honor, glory, power, Wisdom, riches to ob-tain, New do - min - ion ev - ery hour."

APPLEDORE. 8s 7s.

Moderato.

1. Praise to Thee, Thou great Cre-a-tor! Praise to Thee from ev-'ry tongue: Join my soul, with ev-'ry creature, Join the u-ni-ver-sal song.

2. Father, Source of all com-pas-sion, Pure, unbounded love is Thine; Hail the God of our sal-va-tion. Praise Him for His love di-vine.

BARTWELL. 8s & 7s, Double.

E. K. PROUTY.

Moderato.

1. Meek and lowly, pure and ho-ly, Chief among the blessed three, Turning sadness in-to gladness, Heaven-born art thou, Char-i-ty!

2. Hop-ing ev-er, fail-ing nev-er, Tho' deceived, be-liev-ing still; Long a-bid-ing, all-con-fid-ing, To thy heavenly Father's will.

Pity dwell-eth in thy bo-som, Kindness reigneth o'er thy heart; Gentle thoughts a-lone can sway thee, Judgment hath in thee no part.

Never wea-ry of well do-ing, Never fear-ful of the end; Claiming all man-kind as brothers, Thou dost all alike befriend.

ERMINE. 8s & 7s.

ONE BY ONE. 8s & 7s. J. E. GOULD.

FRONDED PALM. 8s & 7s.

KENNETT. 8s & 7s, 6 lines, Peculiar.

1. Hark! ten thou-sand harps and voi-ces Sound the note of praise a-bove: Je-sus reigns, and heaven re-joi-ces; Je-sus reigns, the God of love;

2. King of glo-ry, reign for-ev-er! Thine an ev-er-last-ing crown: Noth-ing from Thy love shall sev-er Those whom Thou hast made Thine own:

3. Sav-ior, hast-en Thine ap-pear-ing; Bring, oh, bring the glo-rious day, When the might-y sum-mons hear-ing, Earth-ly things shall pass a-way.

See, He sits on yon-der throne; Je-sus rules the world a-lone. Hal-le-lu-jah, Hal-le-lu-jah, Hal-le-lu-jah, A-men.

Hap-py ob-jects of Thy grace, Des-tined to be-hold Thy face. Hal-le-lu-jah, Hal-le-lu-jah, Hal-le-lu-jah, A-men.

Then, with gold-en harps we'll sing, "Glo-ry, glo-ry to our King!" Hal-le-lu-jah, Hal-le-lu-jah, Hal-le-lu-jah, A-men.

16

ARCADOME. 8s, 7s & 4s. JOHN MORRISON.

Allegretto.

1. Men of God, go take your stations, Darkness reigns throughout the earth ; Go proclaim among the nations, Joyful news of heavenly birth

2. Go, and when exposed to dangers, Je - sus will your souls defend ; Go, and when 'mid foes and strangers, He will still appear your Friend ;

BRAUN. 8s, 7s & 4s. W. S. B. MATHEWS.

Allegretto.

Bear the tid - ings, Bear the tid-ings, Tell the Savior's matchless worth.

His kind presence, His kind presence Shall be with you to the end.

1. Zion stands with hills surrounded, Zi - on, kept by power di -

2. In the furnace God may prove thee, Thence to bring thee forth more

vine, All her foes shall be confounded, Tho' the world in arms combine ; Happy Zi - on, Happy Zi - on, What a favored lot is thine.

bright, But can nev - er cease to love thee, Thou art precious in His sight ; God is with thee, God is with thee, God thine ev-er- last-ing light.

DELIVERANCE. 8s, 7s, & 4s.   J. M. PELTON. 1868.

OLDS. 8s, 7s, & 4s.   W. IRVING HARTSHORN.

POPULAR TUNES.

HAMDEN. 8s, 7s, & 4s.   Dr. L. Mason, by permission.

Guide me,   O thou great Je - ho - vah, Pil - grim thro' this bar - ren land : } Bread of heav - en. Feed me till I want no more
I am weak, but thou art might - y, Hold me with thy power - ful hand ; }

AMELIA. 8s, 7s, & 4s.   Geo. B. Loomis, From the "Diapason," by permission.

1. { Savior, like a shepherd lead us; Much we need thy ten - der care ;
     In thy pleasant pastures feed us ; [Omit   .   .   .   ] For our use thy folds prepare; Blessed Jesus! Blessed Jesus! Thou hast bought us, thine we are.
2. { Thou hast promised to receive us, Poor and sinful though we be ;
     Thou hast mer - cy to relieve us, [Omit   .   .   ] Grace to cleanse, and power to free; Blessed Jesus! Blessed Jesus! Let us early turn to thee.

ASHCROFT. 8s, 7s & 4s.   From the "Diapason," by permission.

1. In thy name, O Lord, assembling, We, thy people, now draw near. Teach us to rejoice with trembling; Speak, and let thy servants hear,— Hear with meekness,— Hear thy word with godly fear.
2. While our days are earth are lengthened, May we give them, Lord, to thee; Cheered by hope, and daily strengthened, We would run, nor weary be, Till thy glory, Without clouds, in heaven we see.

BILLOW. 8s, 7s, & 4s. Peculiar.   Dr. L. Mason, by permission.

of peace, to wanderers weary, Bright the beams that smile on me; Cheer the pi - lot's vis - ion drea-ry, Far, far at sea,   Far, far at sea.

ARTWELL. 7s & 6s.

Andantino   *FINE.*   *D.C.*

1. { Why sinks my soul de-spond-ing? Why fill my eyes with tears? } Why burdened still with sorrow, Is ev-'ry lab'ring thought?
   { While nature all sur-round-ing, The smile of beauty wears: }

D.C. Each vis-ion that I bor-row, With gloom and sad-ness fraught.

2. { The pleasures that deceived us, My soul no more can charm; } The ob-jects I have cherished, Are emp-ty as the wind;
   { Of rest they have be-reft me, And fill-ed with a-larm; }

D.C. My earthly joys are perished, What com-fort shall I find?

BANNER. 7s & 6s.   P. P. BLISS.

Maestoso   *FINE.*   *D.C.*

1. { Now be the gos-pel ban-ner In ev-'ry land un-furl'd; } Till ev-'ry isle and na-tion Till ev-'ry tribe and tongue,
   { And be the shout ho-san-na Re-ech-oed thro' the world; }

D.C. Receive the great sal-va-tion, And join the hap-py throng

2. { Yes, Thou shalt reign for-ev-er, O Je-sus, King of kings! } The isles for Thee are wait-ing, The deserts learn Thy praise,
   { Thy light, Thy love, Thy fa-vor, Each ransom'd cap-tive sings; }

D.C. The hills and valleys greeting, The song re-spon-sive raise.

BRIDGMAN. 7s & 6s.   A. W. KEEN.

1. Go, when the morning shineth, Go, when the noon is bright; Go when the eve declineth, Go, in the hush of night: Go, with pure mind and feeling, Put earthly thot's a-

2. Remember all who love thee, All who are loved by thee, Pray, too, for all who hate thee, If any such there be; Then for thyself in meekness, A blessing humbly

way,   And in God's presence kneeling, Do thou in secret pray.

claim, And blend with each petition, Thy great Redeemer's name.

HECTOR. 7s & 6s.

1. In heavenly love abiding, No change my heart shall fear, And safe is such con-

2. Wherev-er He may guide me, No want shall turn me back: My Shepherd is be-

tid - ing, For nothing changes here: The storm may roar about me, My heart may low be laid, But God is round about me, And can I be dismayed?

side me, And nothing can I lack; His wisdom ev - er waketh, His sight is never dim; He knows the way He taketh, And I will walk with Him.

AGASSIZ. 6s & 4s.

1. Nearer, my God, to Thee, Nearer to Thee: E'en tho' it be a cross That raiseth me, Still all my song shall be, Nearer, my

2. Tho' like a wan-der-er, Daylight all gone, Darkness be o - ver me, My rest a stone, Yet in my dreams, I'd be Nearer, my

God to Thee, Nearer, my God to Thee, Nearer to Thee.

God to Thee, Nearer, my God to Thee, Nearer to Thee.

BERYL. 6s & 4s.

1. There is a happy land, Far, far away, Where saints in glory stand,

2. Bright in that happy land, Beams ev'ry eye, Kept by a Father's hand,

Bright, bright as day; Oh, how they sweetly sing, Worthy is our Savior King! Loud let His praises ring, Praise, praise for aye.

Love can-not die; Oh, then to glory run! Be a crown and kingdom won; And bright above the sun, We reign for aye.

AMERICA. 6s & 4s. ENGLISH.

1. My country, 'tis of thee, Sweet land of liberty, Of thee I sing: Land where my fathers died; Land of the pilgrim's pride; From ev'ry mountain side Let freedom ring.
2. My native country! thee, Land of the noble free, Thy name I love; I love thy rocks and rills, Thy woods and templed hills; My heart with rapture thrills, Like that above.

ITALIAN HYMN. 6s & 4s. GIARDINI.

Moderato.

Come, thou almigh-ty King, Help us thy name to sing, Help us to praise! Father all glo - ri-ous, O'er all vic - to - rious, Come and reign over us, Ancient of Days.

DORT. 6s & 4s. DR. MASON by permission.

Firmly.

God bless our native land, Firm may she ever stand Thro' storm and night! When the wild tempests rave, Ruler of wind and wave! Do thou our country save, By thy great might.

NOWLIN. 6s & 4s. F. W. ROOT.

Expressively.

1. Low - ly and sol - emn be Thy children's cry to thee, Father di-vine—A hymn of suppliant breath, Owning that life and death, Owning that life and death Alike are thine.
2. O Father! in that hour When earth all succoring power Shall disavow, When spear, and shield, and crown In faintness are cast down, In faintness are cast down, Sustain us thou!

NEW TUNES.

CARYL. 6s & 4.

From *Franz*, by F. W. Root.   Words by James R. Murray.

1. O, Father un-to Thee, Who loveth such as me, I of-fer grateful praise For all my days.

2. For days when I am glad, For days when I am sad, For days of good or ill I praise Thee still.

3. For dear ones given me,
For dear ones now with Thee,
For rough or pleasant ways,
For all my days.

4. For I am in Thy care;
Thy love is everywhere;
Thou, Lord, canst do no ill—
I trust Thee still.

BLOSSOM. 6s & 4s, Peculiar.

1. {Child of sin and sor-row, Filled with dismay, } Heaven bids thee come, While yet there's room; Child of sin and sor-row, Hear and o-bey.
{Wait not for to-mor-row, Yield thee to-day:}

2. {Child of sin and sor-row, Why wilt thou die? } Grieve not that love, Which, from a-bove, Child of sin and sor-row, Would bring thee nigh.
{Come, while thou canst bor-row, Help from on high:}

SORROW. 5s & 3s.

P. P. Bliss.

1. Do not mourn, poor child, Do........ not cry; Thou shalt find re-pose.............. By and by.

2. Struggle with thy pain, Be........ re-signed; Qui-et, by and by,.............. Thou shalt find.

ST. CATHERINES. H. M.

With energy.

H. R. PALMER.
From the "Song Queen," by permission.

1. Ye boundless realms of joy, Exalt your Maker's fame; His praise your songs employ, Above the starry frame; Your voi - ces raise; Ye cher - u -

2. Let them adore the Lord, And praise His holy name, By whose al-might-y word, They all from nothing came; And all shall last, From changes

ELO. H. M.

J. R. MURRAY.

Allegretto.

bim, Ye cherubim and seraphim, To sing His praise.

free, From changes free, His firm decree, Stands ev - er fast.

1. Give thanks to God most high, The u - ni - ver-sal Lord, The sovereign King of

2. How might - y is His hand! What wonders He hath done! He formed the earth and

kings: And be His name adored: Thy mercy, Lord! shall still endure; And ever sure abides Thy word, And ev - er sure a - bide Thy word.

seas, And spread the heavens alone: His power and grace are still the same; And let His name have endless praise, And let His name have end-'ess praise.

CLINTON. H. M.   W. Irving Hartshorn. 1868.

CANEA. H. M.   J. M. Pelton.

17

NASHVILLE. L. P. M.　　　　From "Carmina Sacra" by permission.

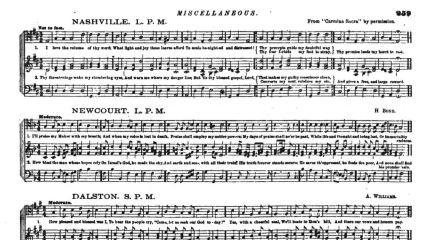

NEWCOURT. L. P. M.　　　　H. BOND.

DALSTON. S. P. M.　　　　A. WILLIAMS.

SINNER COME. 3s & 6s.

Moderato.

1. Sin-ner, come, 'Mid thy gloom, All thy guilt con-fess - ing; Trembling now, Contrite bow, Take the of-fered bless-ing.

2. Sinner, come,
While there's room—
While the feast is waiting;
While the Lord,
By his word,
Kindly is inviting.

SABBATH HOLY. 4s & 7s.

Andante.

Sab - bath ho - ly! To the low - ly, Still thou art a wel-come day, { When thou com-est, earth and o - cean, Shade and brightness, rest and mo - tion, Help the wea - ry heart to pray.

LUCOMBE. 5s & 6s.

Moderato.

1. Lord thyself re - veal, Do thou our sorrows heal, Warm each fro-zen heart, And bless us ere we part.

2. Hear us when we pray,
Drive every doubt away;
Ease each burden'd breast,
In thee may we find rest.

3. Faith and hope increase,
Fill every soul with peace;
Raise our hearts above
And fill us with thy love.

ALCERON. 5s . 7s.

From the "Sabbath Bell" by permission.

1. For-give my fol - ly, O Lord, most ho - ly; Cleanse me from every stain; For thee I languish; Pi - ty my anguish, Nor let my sigh-ing be vain.

2. Deep-ly re - pent-ing, Sore-ly la - ment-ing All my departures from thee; And now re - turn-ing, Thine absence mourning, Lord, show thy mercy to me.

ADA STREET. 6s.

Andantino.

H. W. J.

1. Thy way, not mine, O Lord, How-ev - er dark it be! Lead me by thine own hand; Choose out the path for me.

2. I dare not choose my lot;
   I would not, if I might;
   Choose thou for me, my God,
   So shall I walk aright.

3. The kingdom that I seek
   Is thine: so let the way
   That leads to it be thine,
   Else I must surely stray.

DALNA. 6s.

Allegretto.

G. F. R. From the "Diapason," by permission.

1. Cheer up, de-spond-ing soul! Thy longing pleased I see; 'Tis part of that great whole Wherewith I longed for thee—

2.
To claim thee for my own,
   I suffered on the cross:
Oh, were my love but known,
   All else would be as dross!—

LORD THY WORD ABIDETH. 6s.

Moderate.

G. F. R. From the "Chapel Gems" by permission.

1. Lord, Thy word a - bid - eth, And our footsteps guid - eth! Who its truth be - liev - eth Light and joy re - ceiv - eth.
2. When our foes are near us, Then Thy Word doth cheer us, Word of con - so - la - tion, Mes-sage of sal - va - tion.

3. When the storms are o'er us,
   And dark clouds before us,
   Then its light directeth,
   And our way protecteth.

4. Who can tell the pleasure,
   Who recount the treasure,
   By Thy Word imparted
   To the simple hearted.

SEVERN. 6s & 4s. Peculiar.

Moderate.

From the "Sabbath Hymn and Tune Book" by permission.

{ Far - er yet and pur - er   I would be   in mind, }
{ Dear - er   yet and dear - er   Ev - ery du - ty   find; }   Hop-ing still and trusting God without a   fear, Pa-tient-ly be - liev-ing He will make all clear.

GARLAND WREATH. 6s 8, 10, &4.

Andantine.

1. Whate'er God does is well! His children find it so: Some doth he not with plen-ty bless, Yet loves them not the less; But draws their hearts unto himself a-
2. Whate'er God does is well! In patience let us wait: He doth himself our burden bear, He doth for us take care, And he, our God, knows all our wea-ry

way...... O hearts, o - bey!
days...... O, give him praise!

REINETTE. 7s &3.

Moderate.

{ Jes-us, Sun of righteousness, Brightest beam of love di-vine,
{ With the early morning rays Do thou on our darkness shine, And dispel with purest light All our night!

HEAD OF THE CHURCH. 7s & 4s.

Moderate.

1st time. 2nd time.

Head of the Church tri-umph-ant We joy-ful-ly a - dore thee, Till thou ap - pear thy members here, Still sing like those in glo - ry,
We lift our hearts and voi - ces, With blest an - ti - ci - pa - tion, And cry a - loud and give to God The praise of our sal-(Omit....) va - tion.

WHEN THE VALE. 7s &4.

Moderate. 1st time. 2nd time.

{ When the vale of death appears, Faint and cold this mor-tal clay,
{ Blest Re-deem - er, sooth my fears, Light me thro' the gloomy (Omit) way; Break the shadows, Break the shadows, Ush - er in e - ter - nal day.

KIRKBRIDGE. 8s & 4s.

Maestoso.

1. { Hail! Je - sus! all vic - to - rious Lord! Be thou by all mankind a - dored! }
{ For us didst thou the fight main-tain, And o'er our foes the vic - tory gain, } That we with thee might ev - er reign In end - less day.

UNION DALE. 8s & 4s.   From "Diapason" by permission.

Moderato.

1. Haste, trav'ler, haste! the night comes on, And many a shining hour is gone, The storm is gath'ring in the west, And thou art far from home and rest: Haste, trav'ler haste.
2. The rising tempest sweeps the sky; The rains descend, the winds are high: The waters swell, and death and fear Beset thy path; no refuge near: Haste, trav'ler, haste!

KALMIA. 8s & 4s.   From "Diapason" by permission.

Moderato.

A-las! how poor and lit-tle worth Are all these glittering toys of earth, That lure us here! The dreams of life that death must break, Alas! before it bids us wake, They dis - ap - pear.

Moderato.   **ALCOVE. 8s & 4s.**

2. He breathes—that gentle voice we hear
    As breeze of even:
That checks each fault, that calms each fear,
    That speaks of heaven.

3. And all the good that we possess,
    His gift we own;
Yes, every thought of holiness,
    And victory won.

ILLULA. 8s & 4s.

Moderato.

FINE.

D. C.

{ When the spark of life is wan - ing, Weep not for me;
{ When the lan - guid eye is strain-ing, Weep not for me;
D. C. 'Tis the fet - tered soul's re - leas - ing; Weep not for me.

When the fee - ble pulse is ceas - ing, Start not at its swift de - creas-ing;

SING OF JESUS. 8s & 5.

Moderate.

1. Sing of Je - sus, sing for ev - er Of the love that changes nev - er: Who or what from him can sev - er Those he makes his own?
2. With his blood the Lord hath bought them, When they knew him not, he sought them, And from all their wand'rings brought them; His the praise alone.

THE FLOCK. 8, 8s & 6.

Gently.

1. Shep-herd while the flock is feed - ing, Take these lambs In thine arms, Now for shel - ter plead - ing.

2. While the storm of life is low'ring,
Night and day,
Beasts of prey,
Lurking are devouring.

3. Shepherd, every grace combining,
Keep these lambs
In thine arms,
On thy breast reclining.

REPOSE. 8, 8s &.6.

Cantabile.

G. F. R. From the "Sabbath Bell" by permission.

1. Ere I sleep, for ev - ery fa - vor This day showed By my God, I do bless my Sa - vior.

2. Leave me not, but ever love me;
Let thy peace
Be my bliss,
Till thou hence remove me.

3. And, whene'er in death I slumber,
Let me rise
With the wise,
Counted in their number.

WINONA. 8s & 6s, Peculiar.

1. Let ev-'ry heart re-joice and sing, Let cho-ral an-thems rise; Ye rev-'rend men and chil-dren bring To God your sac-ri-fice;

2. He bids the sun to rise and set; In heaven His power is known. And earth sub-dued to Him shall yet Bow low be-fore His throne:

For He is good, the Lord is good, And kind are all His ways: With songs and hon-ors sound-ing loud, The Lord Je-ho-vah praise

For He is good, the Lord is good, And kind are all His ways: With songs and hon-ors sound-ing loud, The Lord Je-ho-vah praise.

While the rocks and the rills, While the vales and the hills, A glor-ious an-them raise, Let each pro-long the grate-ful song, And the God of our fa-thers praise.

While the rocks and the rills, While the vales and the hills, A glor-ious an-them raise, Let each pro-long the grate-ful song, And the God of our fa-thers praise.

EVENING HOUR. 8s , 6.

Gently.

1. The Sabbath day has reached its close! Yet, Sa-vior, ere I seek re-pose, Grant me the peace thy love bestows— Smile on my even-ing hour!
2. If ev-er I have found it sweet To worship at my Sa-vior's feet, Now to my soul that bliss re-peat—Smile on my even-ing hour!

CAPE RACE. 8s & 6.

Moderato.

From the "Diapason," by permission.

1. Lo! the storms of life are break-ing; Faithless fears our hearts are shak-ing; For our suc-cor un-der-tak-ing, Lord and Sa-vior, help us!
2. Lo! the world, from thee re-bel-ling, Round thy church in pride is swell-ing! With thy word their mad-ness quelling, Lord and Sa-vior, help us!

THE PATRIOT'S PRAYER. 8s & 6s. Double.

Maestoso.

SCOTCH.

1. From foes that would the land de-vour; From guilt-y pride, and lust of power; From wild se - di - tion's law-less hour; From yoke of slav - e - ry; From
2. De - fend, O God, with guardian hand, The laws and rul - ers of our land, And grant thy churches grace to stand In faith and un - i - ty! Thy

blind-ed zeal, by fac - tion led; From gid - dy change, by fan - cy bred; From poisoned er - ror's ser - pent head, Good Lord, preserve us free!
Spir - it's help of thee we crave, That thy Mes - si - ah, sent to save, Re - turn - ing to the world, might have A peo - ple serv - ing thee!

WORK IN GOD'S VINEYARD. 10s & 9s.

B. R. HANBY.

Allegretto.

1. Work in God's vineyard, Je-sus hath call'd thee, Call'd thee from darkness in - to the light; Breaking the chain that long hath en-

2. Faithful thy God hath promised sal - va - tion, Faithful thy load of sor - row He'll bear; Leading the contrite safe thro' temp-

3. Youth, in its ardor, manhood, is glo - ry, In - fan - cy, life's path all yet untrod; . Childhood with dimples, age, with locks

thrall'd thee, Work while the day lasts, and work with thy might.

ta - tion, Up to the mansions He goes to prepare.

hoa - ry, All have a work in the vineyard of God.

SHIELD US. 10s & 4s.

Moderate.

1. Come, Lord, and shield Thy children with thine arm; Re-

2. And grant us peace with - in the church and school, Peace

strain the power of him who seeks our harm: O'er all that would Thy members here as - sail Do Thou prevail, do Thou prevail.

to the powers that our fair country rule, To every wounded conscience aching heart, Thy peace impart! Thy peace impart!

18

FATHER. 11s.

Reverentially.

1. Our Father in heav-en, We hal-low thy name! May thy king-dom ho - ly On earth be the same! Oh, give to us dai - ly Our

2. For - give our transgressions, And teach us to know That hum - ble com - pas - sion Which pardons each foe; Keep us from temp-ta - tion, From

por - tion of bread: It is from thy boun-ty That all must be fed.

e - vil and sin, And thine be the glo - ry For ev - er! A - men!

HELPER. 10s.

Moderate.

1. Rise, crowned with light, im - pe - rial Sa - lem, rise! Ex-

2. See a long race thy spacious courts a - dorn; See

alt thy tower-ing head, and lift thine eyes; See heaven its spark-ling por - tals wide dis - play, And break up - on thee in a flood of day.

fu - ture sons and daughters yet un - born, In crowding ranks on ev - ery side a - rise, De - mand - ing life, im - pa - tient for the skies.

STANDARD TUNES.

277

WHO WILL MEET ME?

From "Chapel Gems."

1. Who will meet me when I die? Who will lead me to the sky? Who will love me in that land? In that spir - it

2. When my Sa - vior from on high? Calls my spir - it to the sky, Who will meet me on the strand Of that spir - it

3. Who will hush my trem-bling heart? Who will heav'n-ly joy im - part? Who will love me in that land? In that spir - it

land? An - gels bright will meet me, An - gels bright, an - gels bright; An - gels bright will meet me, In that spir - it land.

land? An - gels bright will meet me, An - gels bright, an - gels bright; An - gels bright will meet me, In that spir - it land.

land? An - gels bright will meet me, An - gels bright, an - gels bright; An - gels bright will meet me, In that spir - it land.

I WILL SEEK MY FATHER.

Music from Blumenthal, by F. W. Root.

1. When the morn is bright and fair, When sweet song-sters charm the air, I will lift my voice in pray'r, I will seek my Fa-ther;

2. In the sol-i-tude-a-part, In the wil-der-ness or mart, Oh! my sore-ly tempt-ed heart, I will seek my Fa-ther;

3. When the ev'n-ing sun is red, When each blos-som droops its head, Kneel-ing low be-side my bed, I will seek my Fa-ther;

Lest my feet should go a-stray From His pure and per-fect way; Lest I grieve Him as I may, I will seek my Fa-ther.

In the dark-ness as the day, He shall be my Guide and Stay; I will lean on Him al-way— I will seek my Fa-ther.

That I slum-ber in His care, Shield-ed from each harm-ful snare; And for life or death pre-pare; I will seek my Fa-ther.

THE BEACON LIGHT.　From "Chapel Gems."

Andantino.

1. We are sail - ing o'er an o - cean, To a far and for - eign shore, And the waves are dash-ing round us, And we hear the break-ers roar:

2. Tho' the skies are dark a - bove us, And the waves are dash-ing high, Let us look to - ward the bea - con, We shall reach it by and by:

3. He will keep it ev - er burn-ing, From the light-house of his love, And it al - ways shines the brightest When the skies are dark a - bove:

But we look a - bove the bil - lows, In the dark - ness of the night, And we see the stead - y gleam-ing Of our change-less bea-con light.

'Tis the light of God's great mer-cy, And he holds it up in view, As a guide-star to his chil-dren, As a guide to me and you.

If we keep our eyes up - on it, And we steer our course a - right, We shall reach the har - bor safe - ly By the bless - ed bea - con light.

CHORUS.

O, the light is flash-ing brightly, From a calm and storm-less shore, Where we hope to cast our an - chor When our voy - ag - ing is o'er.

A THOUSAND YEARS.

("And they lived and reigned with Christ a thousand years." Rev. xx. 4.)

HENRY C. WORK. By permission.
Words prepared by WM. O. CUSHING.

1. Lift up your head, des-pond-ing Chris - tian, Fling to the winds your need-less fears; Zi-on's bright King, your Guide and. Sav - ior,

2. What if the clouds, one lit - tle mo - ment, Hide the sweet light where morn ap-pears? Bright is the day, where Christ in glo - ry,

CHORUS.

Says you shall reign a thou-sand years. A thou - sand years, my own be - lov - ed! 'Tis the bright day from heav'n un - roll'd;

Says you shall reign a thou-sand years. A thou - sand years, my own be - lov - ed! 'Tis the bright day from heav'n un - roll'd;

'Tis the glad morn, whose fade-less glory, Proph-ets and bards so long fore-told.

'Tis the glad morn, whose fade-less glo - ry, Proph-ets and bards so long fore-told.

3. Strong are the foes thy path surrounding,
Scorning alike thy prayers and tears;
Sweet is the voice of Him whose promise
Says you shall reign a thousand years.
A thousand years, &c.

4. A thousand years! O day of glory!
'Tis the bright star when morn appears;
The herald dawn of blissful ages,
And every day a thousand years.
A thousand years, &c.

JESUS BY THE SEA.—CONCLUDED.

love the pre-cious Word, Which He spake to them that heard, While He taught the wait-ing peo-ple by the sea.

walk'd up-on the wave, His be-lov-ed ones to save, While He brought them safe-ly o'er the storm-y sea.

long to leave my all, At the dear Re-deem-er's call, And His true dis-ci-ple ev-er-more to be.

LOOK AND LIVE.

Moderate.   *Words and Music by* P. P. BLISS.

1. { Look to Je-sus, wea-ry one, Look and live, look and live; Look at what the Lord has done, Look and live; }
   { See Him lift-ed on the tree, Look and live, look and live; Hear Him say, "Look un-to me," Look and live; }

2. { Tho' un-wor-thy, vile, un-clean, Look and live, look and live; Look a-way from self and sin, Look and live; }
   { Long by Sa-tan's power en-slaved, Look and live, look and live; Look to me, ye *shall be saved,* Look and live; }

3. { Tho' you've wan-der'd far a-way, Look and live, look and live; Har-den not your heart to-day, Look and live; }
   { 'Tis thy Fa-ther calls thee home, Look and live, look and live; Who-so-ev-er *will may come,* Look and live; }

CHORUS.

Look! the Lord is lift-ed high, Look to Him, He's ev-er nigh, Look and live, why will ye die? Look and live.

"CHRISTIAN! WALK CAREFULLY."

James R. Murray.

1. Chris-tian! walk care - ful - ly, dan - ger is near! On, in thy jour - ney, with trembling and fear, Snares from with - out, and temp - ta - tion with - in, Seek to en - tice thee a - gain in - to sin. Chris-tian! walk cheer - ful - ly, tho' the fierce storm Dark - en thy sky with the clouds of a - larm, Soon will those clouds and the tem - pest be past, And thou dwell safe - ly with Je - sus at last.

2. Chris-tian! walk hum - bly, ex - ult not in pride; All that thou hast is by Je - sus sup - plied; Hold - ing thee up, he di - rect - eth thy ways. To him be ev - er the glo - ry and praise. Chris-tian! walk stead - fast - ly, while it is light: Swift are ap - proaching the shadows of night, All that thy Mas - ter hath bid - den thee do Haste to per - form, for thy mo - ments are few.

3. Chris-tian! walk prayer-ful - ly, oft wilt thou fall If thou for - get on thy Sa - vior to call, Safe shalt thou walk thro' each tri - al and care, If thou art clad in the ar - mor of prayer. Chris-tian! walk hope - ful - ly, trouble and pain, Cease when the hav - en of rest thou dost gain, This from the lips of the Judge, thy re - ward, "En - ter for - ev - er, the joy of thy Lord!"

THIS IS MY COMMANDMENT.—Concluded.

May thy love u - nite us To the liv - ing Vine. May our hearts en - light - en'd, Glow with love di - vine.

Ev - er - more as breth - ren In sweet u - nion live. As we wish for - give - ness, May we each for - give.

Ev - er meek and low - ly, Ev - er kind and true, Ev - er pure and ho - ly, Paths of peace pur - sue.

This is my com-mand-ment, That ye love one an - oth - er, that ye love one an - oth - er, As I have lov - ed you.

This is my com-mand-ment, That ye love one an - oth - er, that ye love one an - oth - er, As I have lov - ed you.

19

WILL YOU GO?

Words by M. B C. Slade.

1. A voice sweet-ly calls from the shin-ing world a - bove, Will you go? will you go? will you go?.... The dear Lord is call-ing in ac-cents full of love, Will you go? will you go? will you go?..... A - far He sees you and calls you home; His love is waiting for all who come; His love your sor-row and sin can now re-move, Will you go? will you go? will you go?......

2. We've strayed far a-way in the wil - der - ness of sin, Will you go? will you go? will you go?..... Where an-gels are wait-ing to lead the wan - d'rer in, Will you go? will you go? will you go?..... With ten - der mer - cy the Shep-herd stands, To lead you in with His own strong hands; He loves to bring you His lov-ing fold with - in, Will you go? will you go? will you go?......

3. Oh ! come ere life's sun - set has fad - ed in the west, Will you go? will you go? will you go?..... To man-sions pre-par - ing for you a - mong the blest, Will you go? will you go? will you go?..... O'er sin's dark moun-tains no long - er stray, Come walk with us in the *nar-row way That leads a - bove to the hap-py land of rest,* Will you go? will you go? will you go?......

THE BEAUTEOUS DAY.

G. F. R. From "Chapel Gems."

Slow.

1. We are watch-ing, we are wait-ing, For the bright pro-phet-ic day, When the shad-ows, wea-ry shad-ows, From the world shall

2. We are watch-ing, we are wait-ing, For the star that brings the day, When the night of sin shall van-ish, And the shad-ows

roll a - way. We are wait-ing for the morn-ing, When the beauteous day is dawn-ing, We are wait-ing for the morn-ing, For the

CHORUS.

melt a - way. We are wait-ing, &c

gol - den spires of day. Lo! He comes! see the King draw near; Zi - on, shout, the Lord is here.

Lo! He comes, &c.

3. We are watching, we are waiting,
    For the beauteous King of day;
    For the chiefest of ten thousand,
    For the Light, the Truth, the Way.
        We are waiting, &c.

4. We are watching, we are waiting,
    For the bright prophetic day,
    When the shadows, weary shadows,
    From the world shall roll away.
        We are waiting, &c.

OUR BEAUTIFUL HOME.

Words by EMILY HUNTINGTON MILLER.
Music by G. F. R.

1. Be-yond the dark riv-er of death, Be-yond where its wa-ters are swell-ing, The home of my spir-it is

2. No grief in that beau-ti-ful home! No sor-row can en-ter its por-tals! But glad are the voi-ces that

3. No tears in that beau-ti-ful home, No sin from our Sav-ior to sev-er! The King in His beau-ty our

CHORUS.

wait-ing for me, The land where the ran-somed are dwell-ing. No night in that beau-ti-ful home! No

join in its song, The song of the shin-ing im-mor-tals. No night in that beau-ti-ful home! No

eyes shall be-hold, And join in His prais-es for-ev-er! No night in that beau-ti-ful home! No

shade on its glo-ry is seen; The won-der-ful riv-er of wa-ter of life Flows soft thro' the mead-ows of green.

shade on its glo-ry is seen; The won-der-ful riv-er of wa-ter of life Flows soft thro' the mead-ows of green.

AS DOWN IN THE SUNLESS RETREATS.

E. UBAN...

Slowly. ALTO SOLO.

1. As, down in the sun-less re-treats of the o-cean, Sweet flow-ers are spring-ing no mor-tal can see, So,
2. As still to the star of its wor-ship, tho' cloud-ed, The nee-dle points faith-ful-ly o'er the dim sea, So,

deep in my heart, the still prayer of de-vo-tion, Un-heard by the world, ri-ses si-lent to Thee,
dark as I roam, thro' this win-try world shroud-ed, The hope of my spir-it turns trem-bling, to Thee,

ALTO.

My God! si-lent to Thee— Pure, warm, si-lent to Thee
My God! trem-bling to Thee; True, fond, trem-bling to Thee

So, deep in my heart, the still prayer of de-vo-tion, Un-heard by the world, ri-ses si-lent to Thee
So, dark as I roam, thro' this win-try world shroud-ed, The hope of my spir-it turns trem-bling, to

O LOVE THE LORD.—Concluded.

tab - lish, shall es - tab - lish thy heart, All ye who put your trust in the Lord, All ye who put your trust in the Lord.

tab - lish, shall es - tab - lish thy heart, All ye who put your trust in the Lord, All ye who put your trust in the Lord.

SING UNTO THE LORD.   T. M. TOWNE.

- Un - to the Lord,   un - to the Lord, Sing un - to the Lord, O ye saints of his; And give thanks at the remembrance of his

Sing   Sing

Un - to the Lord,   un - to the Lord, Sing un - to the Lord, O ye saints of his; And give thanks at the remembrance of his

SING UNTO THE LORD.—Concluded.

ho - li - ness, Of his ho - li - ness, of his ho - li - ness. Sing un - to the Lord, Sing un - to the Lord,

ho - li - ness, Of his ho - li - ness, of his ho - li - ness. Sing un - to the Lord, Sing un - to the Lord,

Sing un - to the Lord, O ye saints of his, Sing un - to the Lord, O ye saints of his. A - men! A - men!

Sing un - to the Lord, O ye saints of his. A - men! A - men!

OUR SOUL WAITETH:

Our soul wait - eth for the Lord: He is our help and shield, For our heart shall re - joice, shall re-

Our soul wait - eth for the Lord: He is our help and shield, For our heart shall re-

For our heart shall re - joice,

joice in Him, be - cause we have trust-ed in His ho - ly name. Let Thy mer - cy, O Lord, be up - on us, ac-

joice in Him, be - cause we have trust-ed in His ho - ly name. Let Thy mer - cy, O Lord, be up - on us, ac-

cord-ing as we hope in Thee. Let Thy mer - cy, O Lord, be up - on us, ac - cord-ing as we hope in Thee.

cord-ing as we hope in Thee. Let Thy mer - cy, O Lord, be up - on us, ac - cord-ing as we hope in Thee.

BLESSED IS THE PEOPLE.—Concluded.

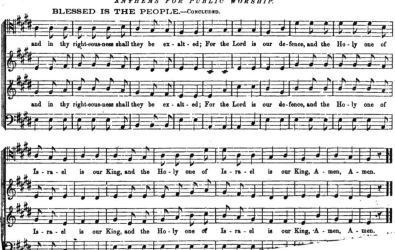

ANTHEMS FOR PUBLIC WORSHIP.

"THOU WILT SHOW ME THE PATH OF LIFE."

From the "New Coronet."

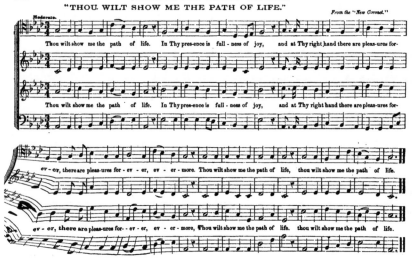

THE LORD IS GOOD.

James R. Murray.

The Lord is good un-to them that wait for Him, To the soul that seek-eth Him; Therefore will I trust in Him, Therefore will I trust in

Therefore will I trust in

The Lord is good un-to them that wait for Him, To the soul that seek-eth Him; Therefore will I trust in Him, Therefore will I trust in

Therefore will I trust in

Him, The Lord is good to them that wait for Him, There - fore will I trust in Him, A - men, A - men.

Him, The Lord is good, the Lord is good, is good to them that wait for Him, Therefore will I trust in Him, will trust in Him, A - men, A - men.

Him, The Lord is good to them that wait for Him, There - fore will I trust in Him, A - men, A - men.

Him, The Lord is good, the Lord is good, is good to them that wait for Him, Therefore will I trust in Him, will trust in Him, A - men, A - men.

BLESS THE LORD.—Concluded.

i - qui-ties, who heal - eth all thy dis - eas - es, Who re - deem-eth thy life from de-struc-tion: Who crown-eth thee with lov-ing

i - qui-ties, who heal - eth all thy dis - eas - es, Who re - deem-eth thy life from de-struc-tion: Who crown-eth thee with lov-ing

kind-ness, who crown-eth thee with lov - ing kind-ness and ten - der mer-cies, Bless the Lord, O my soul, Bless the Lord.

kind-ness, who crown-eth thee with lov - ing kind-ness and ten - der mer-cies, Bless the Lord, O my soul, Bless the Lord.

UNTO HIM THAT LOVED US.

PRAISE THE LORD ALL YE NATIONS.

Will Hill.

O praise the Lord   all ye nations, Praise Him all ye people, praise Him all ye people,   O praise the Lord,

praise Him all ye people, For His mer-ci-ful kindness is great tow'rd us, is great tow'rd us, and the truth of the

Lord en-du-reth for-ev-er, for-ev-er and ev-er,   ev-er and ev-er,   Praise ye the Lord.

GIVE EAR, O SHEPHERD OF ISRAEL.

Give ear, O Shepherd of Is - ra - el, Thou that leadest Joseph like a flock, Thou that dwellest between the cherubims, that

Give ear, O Shepherd of Is - ra - el, Thou that leadest Joseph like a flock, Thou that dwellest between the cherubims, that

dwellest between the cherubims, shine forth, shine forth. Turn us again, O God of Hosts, and cause Thy face to shine upon us, Thy

dwellest between the cherubims, shine forth, shine forth. Turn us again, O God of Hosts, and cause Thy face to shine upon us, Thy

Turn us a - gain, O God of Hosts,

face to shine upon us, and we shall be saved.. and we shall be saved, and we shall be saved.

face to shine upon us, and we shall be saved, Turn us a - gain, O God of Hosts, and we shall be saved, and we shall be saved

THE LORD'S PRAYER.—Concluded.

tres-pass-es, as we for-give them, as we for-give them, as we for-give them that tres-pass a-gainst us. Lead us not in-to temp-ta-tion; but de-

tres-pass es, as we for-give them, as we for-give them, as we for-give them that tres-pass a-gainst us. Lead us not in-to temp-ta-tion; but de-

liv-er us, de-liv-er us from e - vil: For thine is the king-dom, the pow'r and the glo-ry, for-ev-er and ev-er, for ev-er and ev-er.   A - men.

liv-er us, de-liv-er us from e - vil: For thine is the king-dom, the pow'r and the glo ry, for-ev-er and ev-er, for ev-er and ev-er.   A - men.

TEACH ME, O LORD.—Concluded.

to the end; Teach me, teach me, teach me the way, and I shall keep it un-to the end,   I shall keep it un-to the end. A - men.

to the end; Teach me, teach me, teach me the way, and I shall keep it un-to the end,   I shall keep it un-to the end, A - men.

O PRAISE THE LORD.

T. Martin Towne.

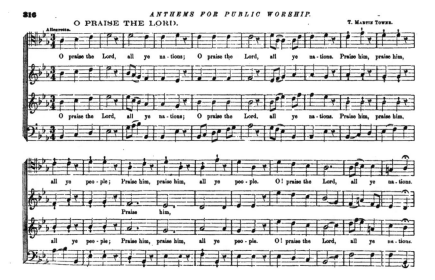

O PRAISE THE LORD.—Concluded.

For his mer-ci-ful kind-ness is great to-ward us, And the truth of the Lord en-dur-eth for-

For his mer-ci-ful kind-ness is great to-ward us, And the truth of the Lord en-dur-eth for-

ev-er! And the truth of the Lord en-dur-eth for-ev-er!   A-men! A-men!

ev-er! And the truth of the Lord en-dur-eth for-ev-er! Praise ye the Lord, A-men! A-men!

PUT ON THE WHOLE ARMOR.—Concluded.

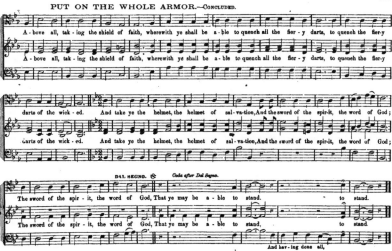

A - bove all, tak - ing the shield of faith, wherewith ye shall be a - ble to quench all the fier - y darts, to quench the fier-y

A - bove all, tak - ing the shield of faith, wherewith ye shall be a - ble to quench all the fier - y darts, to quench the fier-y

darts of the wick - ed.   And take ye the helmet, the helmet of sal - va-tion, And the sword of the spir-it, the word of God ;

darts of the wick - ed.   And take ye the helmet, the helmet of sal - va-tion, And the sword of the spir-it, the word of God ;

DAL SEGNO. 𝄋   *Coda after Dal Segno.*

The sword of the spir - it, the word of God, That ye may be a - ble to stand.   to stand.

The sword of the spir - it, the word of God, That ye may be a - ble to stand,   to stand.

And hav - ing done all,

OH TRUST IN GOD.

J. M. PELTON.
Words from the German.

1. Oh trust in God, the God of our sal - va - tion, Trust in the Lord, to heal our des - o - la - tion! The cause is precious

2. Oh trust in God, the God of earth and o - cean, His cause is safe, though earth were in com - mo-tion; Should floods arise and

in His sight, He has an arm of boundless might, He has an arm of boundless might; Oh trust to God nor yield to fear, Our

tempests roar, And millions threaten to devour, And millions threaten to de - vour; Yet trust in God in Him con - fide, And

help-er is for - ev - er near, Our help-er is for - ev - er near; In darkness as in light, In darkness as in light

in his sa-cred peace a-bide, And in his sa-cred peace a-bide; Who reigns for - ev - er more, Who reigns for - ev - er more.

21

The Ten Commandments.—Concluded.

BLESSED ARE THEY.

Thou shalt not steal, nor false-ly swear, To cov-et thou shalt nev-er dare.

Thou shalt not steal, nor false-ly swear, To cov-et thou shalt nev-er dare.

Bless-ed are they that do his commandments, that

Bless-ed are they that do his commandments, that

they may have right to the tree of life, And may en-ter in thro' the gates in-to the cit-y.

they may have right to the tree of life, And may en-ter in thro' the gates, thro' the gates, in-to the cit-y.

OUR HEAVENLY FATHER.

J. R. GOULD.

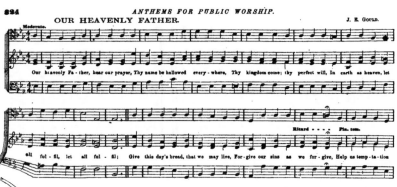

Our heavenly Fa - ther, hear our prayer, Thy name be hallowed every - where, Thy kingdom come; thy perfect will, In earth as heaven, let

all ful - fil, let all ful - fil; Give this day's bread, that we may live, For - give our sins as we for - give, Help us temp - ta - tion

Più Moderato. *Repeat for Amen.*

LOVE YOUR ENEMIES.

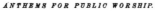

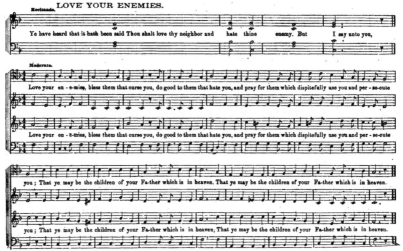

Ye have heard that it hath been said Thou shalt love thy neighbor and hate thine enemy. But I say unto you,

Love your en - e-mies, bless them that curse you, do good to them that hate you, and pray for them which dispitefully use you and per - se-cute

Love your en - e-mies, bless them that curse you, do good to them that hate you, and pray for them which dispitefully use you and per - se-cute

you ; That ye may be the children of your Fa-ther which is in heaven, That ye may be the children of your Fa-ther which is in heaven.

you ; That ye may be the children of your Fa-ther which is in heaven, That ye may be the children of your Fa-ther which is in heaven.

CONSIDER THE LILIES:

Con - sid - er the lil - ies of the field, how they grow. They toil not, they toil not, neither do they spin; And

Con - sid - er the lil - ies of the field, how they grow. They toil not, they toil not, neither do they spin; And

yet I say un - to you, That e - ven Sol - o - mon in all his glo - ry was not ar - ray'd like one............ of these.

yet I say un - to you, That e - ven Sol - o - mon in all his glo - ry was not ar - ray'd like one......... of these.

TEACH ME, O LORD.

F. W. Root.

Teach me, O Lord, the way of thy statutes, and I shall keep it un-to the end. Give me un-der-standing, and

I shall keep thy law; Give me un-der-standing, and I shall keep thy law, and I shall keep thy law: Yes,

Yes, I shall ob-serve it,

I shall ob-serve it with my whole heart, Yes, I shall ob-serve it with my whole heart. A - men, A - men.

O PRAISE THE LORD.—Concluded.

For his mer - ci - ful kind - ness is great to - ward us, And the truth of the Lord en - dur - eth for -

For his mer - ci - ful kind - ness is great to - ward us, And the truth of the Lord en - dur - eth for -

ev - er! And the truth of the Lord en - dur - eth for - ev - er! A - men! A - men!

ev - er! And the truth of the Lord en - dur - eth for - ev - er! Praise ye the Lord, A - men! A - men!

BLESSED AND HOLY.

Moderate.

Bless-ed and ho - ly, Blessed and ho - ly, Blessed and ho - ly is he who has part in the first res - ur - rec - tion, On

Bless-ed and ho - ly, Blessed and ho - ly, Blessed and ho - ly is he who has part in the first res - ur - rec - tion, On

such the sec-ond death hath no power, On such the second death hath no power, but they shall be priests of God and of Christ, they shall be

such the sec-ond death hath no power, On such the second death hath no power, but they shall be priests of God and of Christ, they shall be

priests of God and of Christ, And shall reign with him a thousand years, shall reign with him a thou - sand years. A - men.

priests of God and of Christ, And shall reign with him a thousand years, shall reign with him a thou - sand years. A - men.

BEHOLD! O GOD, OUR SHIELD.—Concluded.

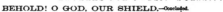

I PRAISE THEE, O LORD, MY GOD.

Arranged from a solo in Mendelssohn's "St. Paul."

I praise thee, O, Lord, my God, with all my heart for - ev - er-more, for-ev - er-more, I praise thee, O Lord, my God, with

more,

I praise thee, O, Lord, my God, with all my heart for - ev - er-more, for-ev - er-more, I praise thee, O Lord, my God, with

my heart for - ev - er more, with all my heart, with all my heart, for - ev - er more ; For great is thy mer - cy to-wards

all

all my heart for - ev - er more, with all my heart, with all my heart, for - ev - er more ; For great is thy mer - cy to-wards

I PRAISE THEE, O LORD, MY GOD.—Concluded.

me, and thou hast de - liv - er - ed my soul from the low-est, from the low-est hell, From the low-est, from the low-est, low - est

low - - - - - - est hell,

me, and thou hast de - liv - er - ed my soul from the low-est, from the low-est hell, From the low-est, from the low-est, low - est

hell; I praise thee, I praise thee, O Lord, my God, with all my heart, for - ev - er-more, O Lord, my God, O Lord, my God, I praise thee.

hell; I praise thee, I praise thee, O Lord, my God, with all my heart, for - ev - er-more, O Lord, my God, O Lord, my God, I praise thee.

22

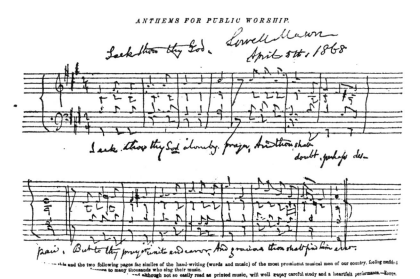

... this and the two following pages fac similes of the hand-writing (words and music) of the most prominent musical men of our country, feeling confiden(t) ... to many thousands who sing their music. ... although not so easily read as printed music, will well repay careful study and a heartfelt performance. —Editor.

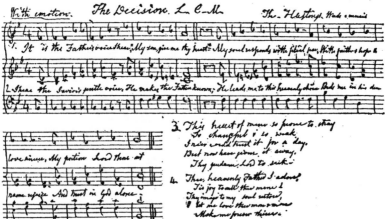

In the letter in which Dr. Hastings kindly responds to our request for a manuscript in his hand writing, he says. "I enclose an original tune and hymn, both written in my eighty-fourth year of age."
The vigor of mind and steadiness of hand here manifested, must strike all with astonishment.—EDITOR.

AS THE HART PANTETH.—Continued.

soul thirsteth for   God,   for the   liv - ing God.

O when shall I   come and ap -

O   when shall I   come and ap - pear be - fore God?

pear be - fore God.

Hope thou in

Why art thou cast down,   O   my soul, And why art thou dis - qui - et - ed with - in   me.

AS THE HART PANTETH.—Concluded.

DAUGHTER OF ZION.

P. P. Bliss.

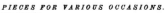

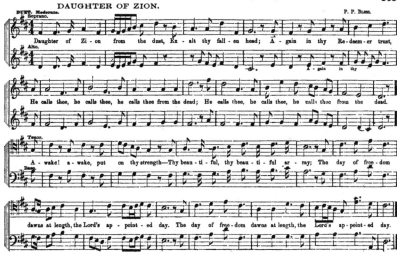

Daughter of Zi - on from the dust, Ex - alt thy fall - en head; A - gain in thy Re - deem - er trust,

A - gain in thy

He calls thee, he calls thee, he calls thee from the dead; He calls thee, he calls thee, he calls thee from the dead.

A - wake! a - wake, put on thy strength—Thy beau - ti - ful, thy beau - ti - ful ar - ray; The day of free - dom

dawns at length, the Lord's ap - point - ed day. The day of free - dom dawns at length, the Lord's ap - point - ed day.

DAUGHTER OF ZION.—Concluded

LET THE HEAVENS REJOICE.—CONCLUDED.

PIECES FOR VARIOUS OCCASIONS.

HOW BEAUTIFUL.

G. F. R. From the "Sabbath Bell," by permission.

How beau-ti-ful up-on the mountains are the feet of him that bringeth good ti-dings, that publisheth peace ; that

saith unto Zi-on, Thy God reign-eth, thy God reign-eth. How beautiful upon the mountains, How beautiful,

The watchmen shall lift up their

voice, to-geth-er shall they sing, For they shall see eye to eye,

How beautiful they sing, How beautiful upon the mountains, how beautiful, When the Lord shall

voice, to-geth-er shall they sing, For they shall see eye to eye.

HOW BEAUTIFUL—Concluded.

bring, shall bring a-gain Zi-on.

Break forth in-to joy, break forth in-to joy,......................

Break forth in-to joy,...................... Break forth in-to joy, Sing, ye waste places

of Je-ru-sa-lem, for the Lord hath comforted his peo-ple; Sing, ye waste pla-ces of Je-ru-sa-lem, Sing, sing to-

geth-er, Sing, sing to-geth-er, for the Lord hath comforted his peo-ple, For the Lord hath comforted his peo-ple. A-men.

PIECES FOR VARIOUS OCCASIONS.

HOW LOVELY IS ZION. Solo and Chorus.

G. F. R. From the "Sabbath Bell" by permission.

HOW LOVELY IS ZION.—Concluded.

Zi - on,...... how love - ly is Zi - on how love - ly! *p*

Joy and peace shall dwell in thee, Joy and peace shall dwell in thee! How love-ly is Zi - on, how love - ly is Zi - on, how

O how love - ly, O how love - ly, Zi - on, cit - y

love - ly is Zi - on, cit - y of our God, How love - ly is Zi - on, how love - ly is Zi - on, how love-ly is Zi - on,

of our God, O how love - ly, O how love - ly is Zi - on, cit - y of our God! A - men.

cit - y of our God. How love-ly, how love - ly, how love - ly is Zi - on! A - men.

28

OH PRAISE THE LORD.

G. F. R.

Oh praise the Lord, ex - alt His name; The boun - ti - ful, the mer - ci - ful, The ev - er bless - ed

Oh praise the Lord, ex - alt His name; The boun - ti - ful, the mer - ci - ful, The ev - er bless - ed

King: Let ev - 'ry voice with loud ac - claim, In thank - ful - ness, and joy - ful - ness His glo - ries sing;

King: Let ev - 'ry voice with loud ac - claim, In thank - ful - ness, and joy - ful - ness His glo - ries sing;

For the bless - ings of the field, For the stores the gar - dens yield, For the joy the har - vests bring,

For the bless - ings of the field, For the stores the gar - dens yield, For the joy the har - vests bring,

OH PRAISE THE LORD.— Concluded.

Oh praise the Lord, ex - alt His name; The boun - ti - ful, the mer - ci - ful, The ev - er bless - ed

Oh praise the Lord, ex - alt His name; The boun - ti - ful, the mer - ci - ful, The ev - er bless - ed

King: Let ev - 'ry voice with loud ac - claim, In thank - ful - ness, and joy - ful - ness His glo - ries sing; In

King: Let ev - 'ry voice with loud ac - claim, In thank - ful - ness, and joy - ful - ness His glo - ries sing; In

thank - ful - ness and joy - ful - ness, In thank - ful - ness His glo - ries sing; A.................men.

His glo.................ries sing.

thank - ful - ness and joy - ful - ness, In thank - ful - ness His glo - ries sing; A - men and a.................men.

His glo.................ries sing.

SHEPHERD OF THINE ISRAEL, LEAD US.—Concluded.

SOFT FLOATING ON THE AIR.—Concluded.

QUARTET. *When singing with the Chorus, very light and distinct.*

Hark! soft float-ing on the air; hark! hark! The ev'n-ing song, The ev'ning song of praise, hark! hark! hark! hark!

Hark! soft float-ing on the air; hark! hark! The ev'n-ing song, The ev'ning song of praise, hark! hark! hark! hark!

The quartet will commence their second and third verses just before the chorus cross, as indicated by the small notes.

CHORUS. *Humming, with mouth shut, to represent distant music.* (*For the ending, let the chorus repeat the last half of the tune without the quartet, a little slower, and dying away.*)

BELLS.

Words by J. R. MURRAY. Music by F. W. ROOT.

Lento Sostenuto.

1. Bells of ear-ly morn-ing, Cheer-i-ly to la-bor call-ing me; From re-fresh-ing slum-ber Do I rise and haste to an-swer thee.

2. Bells of Sab-bath morn-ing, Sooth-ing-ly thy tones sa-lute mine ear, Tell-ing of the Fa-ther, Who to all his own is ev-er near.

3. Bells of Heav'n-ly morn-ing, Sweet-ly call-ing from a storm-less shore, Ye are best and dear-est, Voi-ces of the lov'd ones gone be-fore.

SOFTLY FADES THE TWILIGHT RAY. Quartet, Solo and Chorus.

The first verse is to be sung as a Quartet and the third as a Chorus.

T. Martin Towne.

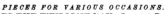

1. Soft - ly fades the twi - light ray, Of the ho - ly Sab - bath day, Gent - ly as, life's set - ting sun, When the Christian's course is run.

3. Sav - ior, may our Sab - baths be, Days of peace and joy in thee; Till in heaven our souls re-pose, Where the sab-bath ne'er shall close.

Solo for Soprano. *Ad Lib.* D. C.

2. Peace is on the world abroad; 'Tis the ho - ly peace of God, Sym - bol of the peace within, When the spir - it rests from sin.

O HOW PURELY. (Trio for Female voices.)

Andantino.

1. O how pure - ly, O how sure - ly, Live the in - no - cent in heart; Ev - er light - ly, Ev - er bright-ly, Every hour doth joy im - part.

2. An - gels standing, where we're wandering, Watch our walk and guard our way; Like the show-ers on the flow - ers, So fall bless - ings all the day.

THOU ART FAIRER.—Concluded.

FREEDOM AND TRUTH.—Concluded.

Freedom and truth! God speed them both! Their banners float unfurled; Their bat-tle-cry has now be-gun To ech-o round the world.

Freedom and truth! God speed them both! Their banners float unfurled; Their bat-tle-cry has now be-gun To ech-o round the world.

TRUTH AND FREEDOM.

1. { He who seeks the truth, and trembles At the dan-gers he must brave, }
   { Is not fit to be a Freeman; He at best is but a Slave. } Be thou like the no-ble Ancients, Scorn the threat that bids thee fear:

D. C. Speak! no mat-ter what be-tide thee; Let them strike, but make them hear.

2. { Be thou like the first A-pos-tles—Be thou like he-ro-ic Paul! }
   { If a free thought seeks expres-sion Speak it bold-ly! speak it all! } Face thine en-e-mies—ac-cus-ers! Scorn the pris-on rack or rod!

D. C. And if thou hast truth to ut-ter, Speak, and leave the rest to God.

UNIVERSITY ANTHEM.

Words by J. M. GREGORY.   Music by G. F. ROOT.

Allegretto.   Written for the inaugural exercises of the Illinois Industrial University.

1. We hail thee! great Fount-ain of learn-ing and light, There's life in thy ra-diance, There's hope in thy might; We

D.C. 4. Then hail thee! blest Fount-ain of learn-ing and light, Shine on in thy glo - ry, rise ev - er in might; We

greet now thy dawn-ing, but what sing - ers' rhyme, Shall fol - low thy course down the a - ges of time. 2. O'er homes of the

greet now thy dawn-ing; but a - ges to come Must tell of thy gran-deur, and shout har-vest home. [*is from here to Coda.*]

mil-lions, o'er fields of rich toil Thy sci - ence shall shine as the sun shines on soil, And Learn-ing and La - bor—fit

head for fit hand, Shall crown with twin glo - ries our broad prai-rie land. 3. And as gen - e - ra - tions, in the

UNIVERSITY ANTHEM.—Concluded.

grand march of time, Shall fill the long a - ges with num - bers sub - lime, Thy por-tals shall throng with the low - ly and

great; Thy sci-ence crowned chil-dren shall bless all the state. We greet now thy dawn - ing, but a - ges to come.

D. C. for fourth verse. Coda after fourth verse.

Must tell............... Must tell...................   Har - vest

of thy gran-deur,   of thy gran-deur,   Must tell of thy gran-deur, and shout, Har-vest home!

home!............. Har - vest home!.............

Har-vest home!   Har-vest home!   Must tell of thy gran-deur, and shout, Har-vest home!   Har - vest home!

24

HE'S GONE. Quartet: IN MEMORY OF WM. B. BRADBURY.   Words and Music by P. P. Bliss.

He's gone,   He's gone,   Gone to the "Si - lent Land."   1. O - ver the "Riv-er of   Death."........
                                                                    2. Close by the "Great White   Throne."........

In - to the "Si - lent Land."   Glad are the "Heav-en - ly   Choirs,"........   Sad is our "Pil - grim   Band."
"Thou-sands of chil - dren   stand."   Wel-come, oh, wel-come," they   sing,..............   "Home to the "Beau-ti - ful   Land."

the " Ev - er-green   Shore,"........   Join-ing the glad "Ju - bi   -   LEE,"........   "Wel-come," the bright an - gels
           our   way,..............   Pil grims and stran-gers we   roam.   Soon shall we join the glad

HE'S GONE.—Concluded.

PRAYER. (Quartet.)

J. M. PELTON.

Andantino.

1. Go, when the morning shineth, Go, when the noon is bright, Go, when the eve de - clin - eth, Go, in the hush of night; Go with pure mind and feel - ing, Put earthly tho'ts a - way, And in God's presence kneel - ing, Do thou in se - cret pray, And in God's presence kneel - ing, Do thou in se - cret pray.

2. Or, if 'tis e'er de - nied thee In sol - i - tude to pray, Should ho - ly tho'ts come o'er thee, When friends are round thy way, E'en then, the si - lent breath - ing Thy spir - it lifts a - bove, Will reach His throne of dwells e - ter - nal love, Will reach that throne of glo - ry, Where dwells e - ter - nal love.

REGNA TERRÆ.

Translated and adapted by G. F. R. From the "Diapason," by permission.

Reg - na ter-ræ can - ta - te, can - ta - te De - o, Reg - na ter-ræ, Psa - li - te, psa - li - te Dom - i - no, Can - ta - te, can - ta - te, can-
All ye na-tions, O sing ye Je-ho-vah's prais-es, All ye na - tions, mag - ni - fy, glo - ri - fy ev-er-more, Sing prais-es, sing prais-es, ex-

ta - te, psa - li - te, Dom - i - no.
alt and mag-ni - fy ev-er-more.

CHORUS.

Reg-na ter-ræ, Can - ta - te De - o, Reg - na ter-ræ, Psa-li - te Dom-i - no, Can-
All ye na-tions, Sing to Je - ho - vah, All ye na-tions, glo - ri - fy ev-er-more, Sing

Reg - na ter-ræ, Can-ta-te, can-ta-te De - o, Reg - na ter-ræ, Psa - li - te, psa-li-te Dom - i - no, Can-
All ye na-tions, O sing ye Je-ho-vah's prais-es, All ye na-tions, mag-ni-fy, glo-ri - fy ev-er-more, Sing

Can - ta - te De - o, Reg-na ter - ræ,
Sing to Je - ho - vah, All ye na - tions,

ta - te, can - ta - te, can - ta - te Dom - i - ne.
prais-es, sing prais-es, sing prais-es to his name.

SOLO. Soprano.

Da - te glo-riam De-o su - per Is-ra-el et su - per coe - los glo-riam, glo-riam e-jus.
Glo - ry give to God a - bove the heav'ns, a-bove the heav'ns, O praise and mag-ni - fy his pow-er.

ta - te, can - ta - te, can - ta - te Dom - i - no.
prais-es, sing prais-es, sing prais-es to his name.

REGNA TERRÆ.—Continued.

REGNA TERRÆ.—Concluded.

OUR DAYS ARE AS A SHADOW.

Our days on the earth are as a sha-dow, and there is none a-bid-ing; We are but of yes-ter-day, of yes-ter-day;

There is but a step be-tween us and death. Man's days are as grass; As a flower of the field, so he

flour-ish-eth, he ap-pear-eth, he ap-pear-eth for a lit-tle time, and then, and then van-ish-eth a-way.

OUR DAYS ARE AS A SHADOW—Concluded.

THE GOD OF ISRAEL.

ROSSINI.

The God of Is - ra - el, The Lord is our Re - deem - - er; God of Ja - cob, de -

sert us not in bat - tle: For the Lord is great in power,

THE GOD OF ISRAEL.—Continued.

And the right-eous he'll de - fend.

Hal-le-lu - jah! Hal-le-

lu - jah! Mag-ni-fy him in the high - est; Hal-le-lu - jah! Hal-le-lu - jah! Magnify him ev-er-

THE GOD OF ISRAEL.—Continued.

more. Sing, Sing, Sing, Sing a-loud, and re-

joice, sing a-loud, and re-joice, sing a-loud, sing a-loud, sing a-loud, and re-

THE GOD OF ISRAEL.—Continued.

joice, sing, sing, and re - joice, sing, sing, and re - joice, re - joice, re - joice, re - joice, re-

- - loce.

- joice. Of - fer him the sac - ri - fice of gladness, Of - fer him the sac - ri - fice of

THE GOD OF ISRAEL.—Concluded.

gladness: He will re - ward thee with his bless - ing; O sing praises un - to his name: Of - fer him the

2d time end here, and return to the beginning. 1st time only.

sac-ri-fice of glad - ness; O sing prai - ses un - to his name: He will re - ward thee with his bless - ing;

THE LORD IS GREAT.

Larghetto Maestoso. RIGHINI.

THE LORD IS GREAT—Continued.

The Lord is great,   the Lord is great, and greatly to be prais-ed,   great-ly to be prais-ed; Who shall not fear his name?

The Lord is great,   and great-ly to be prais-ed, great-ly to be prais-ed; Who shall not fear his name?

The Lord is great,   and great-ly to be prais-ed, great-ly to be prais-ed; Who shall not fear his name? All

The Lord is great,   and great-ly to be prais-ed, great-ly to be prais-ed; Who shall not fear his name?

all nations shall come, shall come and worship him, and glo-ri-fy his name. Who shall not fear Him? Who shall not fear Him?

all nations shall come and wor - ship him, and glo-ri-fy his name. Who shall not fear Him? Who shall not fear Him?

nations, all nations shall come and worship him, and glo-ri-fy his name. Who shall not fear Him? Who shall not fear Him?

and wor . . . . ship, worship him, and glo-ri-fy his name Who shall not fear Him? Who shall not fear Him?

THE LORD IS GREAT—Continued.

Bless - ed is the peo - ple that know the joy-ful sound, Bless - ed is the peo - ple that know the joy-ful sound. They shall ev - er

Bless - ed is the peo - ple that know the joy-ful sound, Bless - ed is the peo - ple that know the joy-ful sound.

They shall

walk, They shall ev - er walk, They shall ev - er walk in the light, in the light of his

They shall ev - er walk in the light of his coun - tenance, shall ev - - - er walk in the light............ of his........

walk, shall ev - er walk, shall ev - er, ev er walk in the light, the light of his

THE LORD IS GREAT—Continued.

coun - te-nance.

coun - te-nance.

coun - te-nance.

In his name shall they re - joice, and in his right-eous-ness shall be ex - alt - - - ed! He is their

shall they re - joice, and in his right-eous-ness shall be ex - alt - - - ed! He is their

In his name shall they re - joice, and in his right-eous-ness shall be ex - alt - - - ed! He is their glo - ry.

THE LORD IS GREAT—Continued.

THE LORD IS GREAT—Continued.

THE LORD IS GREAT—Concluded.

The Ten Blessings.

1. Blessed are the poor in spirit: for | theirs is the | kingdom of | heaven.
2. Blessed are they that mourn : for | they shall be | comfort- | ed.
3. Blessed are the meek : for | they shall in- | herit the | earth.
4. Blessed are they which do hunger and thirst after righteousness: for | they | shall be | filled.
5. Blessed are the merciful: for | they shall ob- | tain | mercy.
6. Blessed are the pure in heart : for | they shall | see | God.
7. Blessed are the peace-makers : for they shall be | called the | children of | God.
8. Blessed are they which are persecuted for righteousness' sake: for | theirs is the | kingdom of | heaven.
9. Blessed are ye, when men shall revile you, and persecute you, and shall say all manner of evil against you, falsely | for | my | sake.
10. Rejoice, and be exceeding glad ; for great is your reward in heaven : for so per- secuted they the | prophets which | were be- | fore you.

I will lift up mine eyes.

1. I will lift up mine eyes unto the hills from whence   cometh   my   help.
2. He will not suffer thy foot to be moved. He that { keepeth thee   will   not   slumber.
3. The Lord is thy keeper, the Lord is thy shade upon thy right.....   hand
4. The Lord shall preserve thee from all evil, He shall pre-serve   thy   soul.

My help cometh from the Lord which made   heaven and   earth.
Behold, He that keepeth Israel shall neither   slumber nor   sleep.
The sun shall not smite thee by day, nor the   moon   by   night.
The Lord shall preserve thy going out and thy com- ing in from this time forth, and even for   { ev - er - more.

O, Sing unto the Lord. L. L. L.

Chant.

1. O sing unto the Lord a new song ; sing unto the Lord   all   the   earth.
2. Sing unto the Lord, bless his name ; show forth his salvation from   day   to   day :

Response.   Chant.

Praise   ye   the   Lord.   3. Declare his glories among the heathen, his wonders a-
Praise   ye   the   Lord.

Response.

mong   all | people: Praise   ye   the   Lord   in   his   ho- | ly   tem - ple.

4. For the Lord is great, and greatly to be praised ; he is to be feared a- | bove all | gods: } Praise ye the Lord.
5. For all the gods of the nations are idols; but the | Lord made the | heavens: } Praise ye the Lord.
6. Honor and majesty are before him; strength and beauty are | in his | sanctuary :   } Praise ye the Lord in his holy temple.

7. Give unto the Lord, O ye kindreds of the people, give unto the Lord | glory and | strength.   } Praise ye the Lord.
8. Give unto the Lord the glory due unto his name; bring an offering and come in- | to his | courts: } Praise ye the Lord.
9. O, worship the Lord in the beauty of holiness; fear be- fore him | all the | earth.   } Praise ye the Lord in his holy temple.

10. Let the heavens rejoice, and let the | earth be | glad: } Praise ye the Lord.
11. Let the sea roar, and the | fullness there- | of :   } Praise ye the Lord.
12. Let the field be joyful, and all that | is there- | in :   } Praise ye the Lord in his holy temple.

13. Then shall all the trees of the wood rejoice be- | fore the | Lord :   } Praise ye the Lord.
14. For he cometh, for he cometh to | judge the | earth: } Praise ye the Lord.
15. He shall judge the world with righteousness, and the | people with his | truth: } Praise ye the Lord in his holy temple.

The Lord is my Shepherd

1. The Lord is my Shepherd, I | shall not | want:
He maketh me to lie down in green pastures; he leadeth me be- | side the | still — | waters.

2. He restoreth my soul; he leadeth me in the paths of righteousness, for his | name's | sake.
Yea, though I walk through the valley of the shadow of death, I will fear no evil; for thou art with me, thy rod and thy | staff, they | comfort | me.

3. Thou preparest a table before me in the presence of mine enemies; thou anointest my head with oil, my | cup runneth | over.
Surely goodness and mercy shall follow me all the days of my life, and I shall dwell in the | house of the | Lord for- | ever, _Ps. xxiii._

God, be Merciful unto Us.

1. God be merciful unto | us, and | bless us,
And cause his | face to | shine up- | on us.

2. That thy way may be | known upon | earth,
Thy saving | health a- | mong all | nations.

3. Let the people | praise thee, O | God;
Let | all the | people | praise thee.

4. O let the | nations be | glad,
And | sing — | for — | joy:

5. For thou wilt judge the people | righteous- | ly,
And govern the | nations up- | on — | earth

6. Let the people | praise thee, O | God;
Let | all the | people | praise thee.

7. Then shall the earth | yield her | increase;
And God, even | our own | God, will | bless us.

8. God will | bless — | us:
And all the ends of the | earth shall | fear — | him. _Ps. lxvii._

O come, let us Sing.

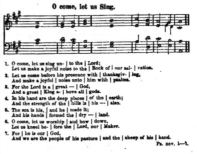

1. O come, let us sing un- | to the | Lord;
Let us make a joyful noise to the | Rock of | our sal- | vation.

2. Let us come before his presence with | thanksgiv- | ing,
And make a joyful | noise unto | him with | psalms.

3. For the Lord is a | great — | God,
And a great | King a- | bove all | gods.

4. In his hand are the deep places | of the | earth;
And the strength of the | hills is | his — | also.

5. The sea is his, | and he | made it;
And his hands | formed the | dry — | land.

6. O come, let us worship | and bow | down,
Let us kneel be- | fore the | Lord, our | Maker.

7. For | he is our | God,
And we are the people of his pasture | and the | sheep of his | hand. _Ps. xcv. 1—7._

Make a Joyful Noise.—*May be sung to the above Chant.*

1. Make a joyful noise unto the Lord, | all ye | lands;
Serve the Lord with gladness, come be- | fore his | presence with | singing.

2. Know ye that the Lord | he is | God:
He hath made us, and not we ourselves; his people, and the | sheep — | of his | pasture.

3. Enter into his gates with thanksgiving, into his | courts with | praise;
Be thankful unto | him, and | bless his | name.

4. For the Lord is good; his mercy is | ever- | lasting,
And his truth en- | dureth to | all gener- | ations. _Ps. c._

Pass Over to thy Rest.

J. K. GOULD.

DUET AD LIB.

```
1. From this bleak | hill of | storms, | To yon warm | sun-ny | heights,
2. From hunger | and from | thirst, | From toil and | weari - | ness,
3. From tides, and | winds, and | waves, | From shipwrecks | of the | deep,
4. From falsehoods | of the | age, | From broken | ties and | hearts,
5. From this un - | anch-ored | world, | Whose morrow | none can | tell,
```

CRES.

```
Where love for - | ev - er | shines,        The rest of | God!
From shadows | and from | dreams,           The rest of | God!
From parted | anch-ors | here,              The rest of | God!
From suns gone | down at | noon,            The rest of | God!
From all things | rest-less | here,         The rest of | God!
```

Pass over to thy | Rest,   the | rest   of | God!

How lovely are thy Tabernacles.

```
1. How lovely are thy | taber- | nacles,
   O | Lord — | of — | hosts.
2. My soul longeth, yes, even fainteth for the | courts of the | Lord :
   My heart and my flesh crieth | out for the | living | God.
3. Yea, the sparrow hath | found an | house,
   And the swallow a | nest | for her- | self ;
4. Where she may | lay her | young :
   Thine altars, O Lord of Hosts, my | King— | and my | God.
```

```
5. Blessed are they that | dwell in thy | house :
   They will | still be | praising | thee.
6. Blessed is the man whose | strength is in | thee,
   In whose | heart | are the | ways.
7. Who passing through the vale of weeping | make it a | well :
   The early rain also doth | cover | it with | blessings.
8. They go from | strength to | strength ;
   Every one appeareth be- | fore— | God in | Zion.
```

"Not my will, but Thine."

W. IRVING HARTSHORN.

```
1. "Thy will not, mine," O gracious Lord, My burdened. | spir - it | cries,
2. Eternal wisdom cannot err, Nor goodness            be | un - | kind,
3. Then should I crave some seeming good, And thou shouldst | deem it | ill,
4. Thus o'er my sorrow-clouded way The bow of | peace shall | shine,
5. And when—O blissful thought—I find In heaven un - | bro - ken | rest,
```

```
Though oft upon my saddened way   Grief's | tear drops | fill  my | eyes.
And thou who art thyself the light  A - | lone canst | lead the | blind.
In mercy, Lord, the gift with-hold      And | bid my | heart be | still.
And faith shall aid me still to say,   "Thy | will be | done, not | mine."
I shall not only know but see         Thy | way, not | mine was | best.
```

Nearer to thee.

C. M. WYMAN.

```
Nearer, my God, to thee, Near- | er to | thee :
Ev'n though it be a cross That | raiseth | me,
Still all my song shall be, Nearer, my | God, to | thee, | Nearer to | thee.
```

GENERAL INDEX OF TUNES.

HYMNS, ANTHEMS, SELECT PIECES AND CHANTS.

METRICAL INDEX OF TUNES.

SINGING SCHOOL AND CONCERT MUSIC.

INDEX OF FIRST LINES.